FAITH AND THE ADOLESCENT

FAITH AND THE ADOLESCENT

PIERRE BABIN

HERDER AND HERDER

1965
HERDER AND HERDER NEW YORK
232 Madison Avenue, New York 10016

Translated by David Gibson.
Original edition: *Dieu et l'adolescent*
(Éditions du Chalet, Lyons 1963).

Nihil obstat: Patrick A. Barry
                  Censor Librorum

Imprimatur: Patrick C. Brennan
                  Vicar General, Diocese of Burlington
                  November 4, 1964

Library of Congress Catalog Card Number: 65-13491
© 1965 by Herder and Herder, Incorporated
Printed in the United States of America

CONTENTS

FOREWORD

In his earlier book, *Crisis of Faith*, Father Babin gave us an intriguing socio-psychological outline of the growth of the religious sense in the adolescent, making certain applications to contemporary catechetical theory and technique. In this present volume, the author expands his treatment and speculates still more deeply about the fusion of the adolescent psyche with the world of salvation history.

The sum total of his writing gives the theorist, the counselor, and the catechetist-in-the-field a fine body of solid facts and honest conjecture with which to approach his complex and elusive subject. While the neophyte will find many helpful insights in these pages, the reader, ideally, should have some previous knowledge of at least the basic dynamics of personality development, particularly in psycho-sexual areas. Such background information seems to be presumed by the author as he sketches what might be called the "genetics of religious growth."

And how beautifully Father Babin dovetails individual psychological progression with the evolution of the religious sense—linking early childhood with notions of creation and the moral order, adolescent friendship with God the Father through Christ his Brother, and the Pentecostal involvement of the adult through a growing life in the Spirit. "The human developmental process calls for progressive growth in the life of grace," Father Babin reminds us. And yet the reverse so often seems to be the case if external behavior tells us anything. How many devoted teachers and parents have watched with dismay as their teenage youngsters— particularly the boys—seem to lose interest in the familiar old religious landmarks. Three years before, their shining, contented faces were prominent in the front pews of our churches, surveying the liturgical mysteries with wide-eyed interest, even enthusiasm! But as the puzzles and adventures of puberty enmeshed them, their spiritual interests receded. Further and further back they sat, then stood in passive, self-conscious little groups, first along the side, then in the rear, finally out in the vestibule and on the steps. Some, eventually, appeared no more.

An even more familiar story is "France pagan." Indeed, it was the empty churches and the amoral ethics of a generation ago that kindled the kind of research which Father Babin writes about. Perhaps it was the earlier defections of the European masses which led to present speculations and experiments by Christian educators on the Continent which are not yet typical of the American approach.

What attitudes seem to characterize the religious guidance of the adolescent in America? One group continues to reflect the inhibiting and anxious traditions of our Yankee-Puritan, Irish-Jansenist past. Adolescence is seen as a "dangerous age" because the adolescent is at heart a natural man, open to sense experience, keen to go his own way, consumed with that "rage to live" about which Father Babin writes with such accuracy and eloquence. The repressed and fearful adult repudiates this developmental phase. Emotions are to be immediately contained (which often means stifled or ignored), and the alarmist calls for more firmness, more discipline, more supervision and outside direction. The result, of course, is that the adolescent feels even more ill-at-ease, more lonely, and more hostile. He rejects these adults who "don't understand," goes emotionally underground, and becomes inaccessible to those who might otherwise have helped had they remained more open and accepting.

A more sympathetic guidance approach acknowledges the adolescent's unique readiness for feeling. The growth of existential schools of education and client-centered counseling have enabled an increasing number of teachers and guides to face the adolescent as he is—with his preoccupation with subjective values, his unpredictable mood swings, his impatience for autonomy, and his immersion in the world of experience. What is often missing, however, is the intuition and skill which will help the adolescent to go beyond these often narcissistic preoccupations to mature and objective religious goals. In other words, we have sometimes become so tolerant of the vital present, that we reflect indifference about all future promise.

Father Babin, in the pages that follow, gives us a fine, panoramic balance. He appreciates, as few other religious writers have, the enormous fixation of the adolescent upon the absorbing world of his emerging self. He has even coined a word—"naturation"—which describes, without belittling, that "plunge into nature through the instincts" which is the homage the typical teenager pays to "the god's in one's blood."

Because Father Babin is able to say an unqualified "yes!" to the inherently volatile and self-centered aspects of the newly pubescent youth, he is also able to lament the tragedy of those who remain rooted for a lifetime on such purely subjective levels. He asks us to accompany the adolescent with compassionate optimism through this self-centered and chaotic passage to adulthood, aware that for the moment all creation and God himself are to be understood chiefly in terms of inner needs and sensate gratifications. Then, having survived these shoals and shallows together, he suggests we plumb, in deeper but calmer waters, those more profound and ultimate aspects of God's Good News which far transcend man's measure of himself.

In *Faith and the Adolescent,* many familiar themes are revisited in the light of new data and fresh insights. Psychosexual development, while less extensively treated than one might wish, is touched upon with good effect. Particularly helpful is the notion that the young male, bombarded as he is by so many sensual stimuli, seeks to "de-corporealize" his religious life at least by dwelling upon those attributes of the Almighty which define him as the all-powerful, *Pure Spirit.* The teenage girl, on the other hand, seems much more ready to approach God as a loving Friend and Confidant, as she searches for the comforting Father-figure she continues to need.

How to help boy and girl alike to accept purity, not as a negation, but as "a personal discovery of the Incarnation" is one of the highlights of the text. This awareness, so crucial to every facet of maturity and holiness, seems an ideal way to extend the incarnational concept to all of life, building a dynamic dependence on God the Creator "which allows them to collaborate in this creative action with an active consent by which they become fully alive." "The glory of God is man fully alive!" This is the leitmotiv which runs through all that Father Babin has written. It is for him not just a description but an invitation, a call to that joy, grace, and fulfillment for which the adolescent yearns —and which the rest of us yearn to give him—through Christ our Lord.

GEORGE HAGMAIER, C.S.P.
Paulist Institute for Religious Research

What are the major characteristics of adolescent faith and what causes them? How does the adolescent's faith evolve? What can be done to help the adolescent through his crisis of faith? This study, based on the responses of 1800 adolescents to the question: "For you, what is God?" is an attempt to cast some light on these difficult questions.

However this presentation is not limited to the statistical results of the inquiry, though the importance of these statistics cannot be overstressed. The observations and experiences of educators, as well as the fields of psychopedagogy and sociology, have also influenced the interpretations.

This study will go beyond a mere inventory of the adolescent's way of expressing God and its motivations. An attempt will be made to penetrate not the total and profound reality of his relationship with God (which touches the mystery of grace), but the great lines of his sense of God, that is, the objective and apparent characteristics of his relationship with God. Moreover some value judgment will be attempted of the content of the adolescent's religious experience in relation to the understanding which the

Church, in her adult consciousness, has of the God of revelation.

This is, therefore, a synthetic essay on the religious mentality of the adolescent, taking into consideration his psychology, his place in the world, and his education. It is an effort to reflect on the place and significance of adolescence in growth toward adult faith, an attempt to rethink psychological matters in the light of Christian revelation. Finally, there is some consideration given to some educational orientations which may benefit the modern adolescent.

1. RELIGIOUS INTERPRETATION AND ADOLESCENT PSYCHOLOGY

Is religious psychology a legitimate field of study? In order to answer this question a distinction must be made on the one hand between the collection of data and their interpretation, and on the other hand between a natural interpretation and an interpretation in the light of faith. A discussion of these distinctions, which in fact represent three levels of reflection and labor, should prove illuminating.

COLLECTION OF DATA

To begin with, this study was aimed at data, the 1800 responses to an inquiry.[1] These responses reveal observable dimensions of religious behavior. They allow us to study how the sense of God for Christian adolescents is manifested and how it develops. Now on this level, which is a sounding of data, there is no reason that this study

[1] The inquiry was conducted by the Centre de Recherche de Psycho-Pédagogie Religieuse de l'Adolescence, a joint project of the Ecole Franco-Canadienne, Sainte Foy-les-Lyon (Rhône), and the Direction de l'Enseignement Religieux, Lyon. The students, ranging in age from 13 to 20, were divided as follows:

should be unacceptable. For believers as well as unbelievers, it is as acceptable as any study in experimental psychology.

NATURAL INTERPRETATION

Second, an effort was made to interpret these data. Not only did we consider the discovered constants, but in addition, we interpreted these constants in an effort to determine what motivations underlay the data. The first step was a natural interpretation attempting to discover the natural psychological and sociological motivations for each type of response. For example, when human dependence on a father is linked with the notion of God the Father, a natural interpretation is made.

What is the value of such natural interpretations? When it has been possible to control them experimentally, according to commonly admitted criteria (such as the law of averages), a scientific interpretation can be claimed. When these interpretations depend on the constants of experiences (as is frequently the case here), or on subjective evidence (as is the case in psychoanalysis), they will

	Parochial School		Public School		Vocational School	
	Boys	Girls	Boys	Girls	Boys	Girls
Preadolescent	100	100	100	100	100	100
Adolescent	100	100	100	100	100	100
Late Adolescent	100	100	100	100	100	100

The complete questionnaire given to the 1800 students can be found in the Appendix. Also given in the Appendix is a preliminary questionnaire given to two hundred students and later abandoned, but occasionally referred to in this book.

more often appear as propositions rather than as true conclusions. Therefore we must pay close attention to the interpretations proposed. Generally they are not proposed
as certitudes, but as general guidelines in our effort to
obtain a better understanding of man.

INTERPRETATION IN THE LIGHT OF FAITH

Third, an attempt was made to interpret these data in the
light of faith. Those Christians who first studied the data
and their natural meaning discovered another significance
going deeper than the first interpretation. This was not
merely the result of natural insight, but was rather the
outcome of a new and original insight through faith.

No attempt was made to systematize this interpretation.
However, in order to understand the Christian import of
man's subjective progress in adherence to God, in order to
understand the providential meaning of different stages,
it is necessary to *view these stages from God's perspective*.
This God-like view can in no way be the result of purely
human reflection. To attain a Christian interpretation of
these data, reason must be aided by the light of revelation.

The Catholic knows that he can find revelation in the
Church's reflection on her own history, which is a history
of a God who intervenes and saves. As expressed by the
Church, this history of salvation reveals that God has intervened in an objective and observable manner in the
course of human events. It is this intervention which manifests a certain God-view, a way of seeing things which is
God-like. It is in systematically studying God's relations

with man in the different moments of history that God's way of viewing man will be understood.

On the human level a young man's regard for a girl is manifested by the way he treats her, speaks to her, and habitually comports himself with her. . . . God reveals his views of man in the same way, by the way he treats him and reacts to his behavior.

This does not mean that we shall pursue the meaning of human states by trying to see how God behaved with adolescents in the Bible. Assuredly this would be most helpful. But rather than follow this course we shall instead study God's *general* way of acting with man, in order to determine, through reflection, the way he views human states and behavior. Thus by reflecting with the Church on God's action with David, Moses, the Pharisees, children, and above all with his Son, we shall come to know what God does and does not love, and how he deals with natural values such as the thirst for happiness, human vitality, and earthly failure. This "frequentation" of God's manner of seeing and doing will little by little reveal the great lines of a Christian vision of man, his states, and his future destiny.

Two Modes of Interpretation

The Christian who attentively reads the responses of these young people interprets them in two ways, namely through reaction and through "comprehension" in the etymological sense of the word.

On the one hand he measures "the infinite distance" which separates the Church's understanding, in her adult consciousness, of the God of revelation (an understanding expressed by theologians and attested and lived by the saints), from that of adolescents. How can the shortcomings and aberrations of these young people be tolerated? Here the believer is led to take up the cry of the prophets: "There is no one who knows God." And he denounces the adolescent's limitations, platitudes, sins and deviations. But as a corollary, such a vision of things can lead to a pedagogy of "purification" and of the "redemption."

On the other hand, more as teacher than prophet, the Christian is led to consider the providential meaning of different stages, conditions and even difficulties in relation to a mature and authentic sense of God. God calls every person by his name, allows both the good and the bad grain to grow for the sake of the good, and leads man into the desert after he has seen the glitter of the promised land. The believer perceives all this and perceives the link between the stages on the road and the end to be attained, between groping and achievement, between the temporal unfolding of human freedom and its perfection in full adherence to God. Here the believer does not denounce, but understands realities as stages, shadows or beginnings. He points to the interior of these realities, the ways of the Spirit nourishing the body of Christ toward full stature. Such a vision demands a pedagogy of the creation and the incarnation, that is, a pedagogy which surpasses existing values, a pedagogy of the assumption.

If one is to be true to the faith, both these complementary modes of interpretation are necessary.

Value of This Interpretation

Insofar as a faith-interpretation is based on data and natural meanings, it is dependent on the seriousness of that basic study. It is necessary, therefore, to stress the dangers and inconsistencies to be met if one proceeds too directly and immediately to interpretations of faith, especially the faith of adolescents.

Second, a faith-interpretation is always addressed to the faith of the reader and thus to his understanding enlightened by the Holy Spirit in the Church. This interpretation is nothing other than a proposition from one believer to another in the Church. Thus there is no question here of an interpretation having the value of dogma. Yet insofar as one's faith is authentic, that is, faithful to the demands of reason as well as to God, the interpretation does not become an illuminism either. It acquires true value as a proposition capable of rousing and enlightening the understanding of the reader.[2]

Meaning of Psychological Terms Applied to Religious Reality

The occasion to speak of religious realities (which, for a Christian, are in themselves supernatural realities) will

[2] For this reason the faith-interpretation should always be prudent and docile to the views of the Church. What prudence she manifests when she uses her authority to canonize a man! A fortiori we must be prudent in the interpretations we propose. It should be noted that if we interpret, we never judge. In particular, we never claim to discern explicitly the ontological reality of grace in a type of behavior.

often arise in connection with psychological realities, as for example, "adult faith."

Those who use such terminology do not always agree on exact meanings. Some are influenced by a canonical, scriptural or sacramental terminology. Others are more influenced by the perspectives of ascetical theology or of psychology. In this book there is no claim to open or respond to a debate, but only to define the use of such terminology in the present context.

A psychological term used in connection with a supernatural reality indicates the psychological (and uniquely psychological) dimension in which the supernatural reality unfolds. Thus, when adult faith is spoken of, by that we mean a life of faith which is manifested and expressed according to such psychological characteristics of adult maturity as freedom, unity, etc. However this designation in no way prejudges the supernatural reality of the faith, the "degree" of faith underlying external conduct. Thus it would be possible for a Christian to possess a high degree of faith or supernatural charity which would be manifested in a psychologically egocentric manner.[3] However, one could also manifest an apparently mature life of faith with a relatively minimal "degree" of faith.

If it may seem that there are too many distinctions here, it would be well to remember that in such a sphere and because of the demands of the study, precise distinctions are necessary to avoid possible ambiguity.

The importance of this can be illustrated with an example. A baptized and confirmed child normally expresses

[3] We must distinguish the meaning of "egocentrism," which has nothing to do with "egoism."

his religious life in an infantile psychological manner, that is, incompletely, egocentrically, in a way dependent on parents, etc. In this case, what could the word "adult" signify on the religious level?

If the word "adult" were used to characterize the fullness of sacramental "character" in the Church, it could be said that the child spoken of above was an adult even if he were only 5 years old. Although this analogy has some value, its ambiguity would lead to confusion in the present discussion of psychological realities. This more sacramental and canonical vocabulary will not be used in this discussion.

If the word "adult" were used to indicate a complete response to God's call, the 7-year-old child could be considered an adult believer insofar as he is subjectively completely faithful to God. But what would be the objective criterion for such a reality? And why use a word with such a definite psychological connotation? This more spiritual and subjective manner of speaking must also be rejected here.[4]

If the word "adult" were used to characterize the adult state of consciousness and freedom in which the life of faith is expressed, it would certainly not be applicable to a 7-year-old child. This will be the use of the term "adult" in the present study, for it will avoid any prejudgment of the sacramental status or holiness of those to whom it is applied.[5]

Such distinctions and definitions do not express revealed

---

[4] Here we would prefer to speak of holiness.

[5] One could find another meaning for the word "adult" by referring to St. Paul's expression "full stature" in Christ. However this meaning has not been retained because it seems to contain all the others and to express eschatological fulfillment.

absolutes, but are the result of a choice in vocabulary required to avoid ambiguity. Psychological disposition and religious reality are neither on the same level nor are they equivalent. But it is true that the distinction of the two orders does not obviate all relationship between them. While affirming the transcendence of supernatural realities in relation to their psychological conditions, the interaction between them is not denied. The reality of grace calls for and gives birth to a perfecting of psychological dispositions as well as a healing of psychic deviations. But then, too, the human developmental process calls for progressive growth in the life of grace.

2. THREE MAJOR CHARACTERISTICS OF THE SENSE OF GOD AMONG ADOLESCENTS

THE COURSE OF THIS STUDY

There are three important processes which seem to characterize the sense[1] of God among adolescents. These are naturation, egomorphism and the ethical sense. It was necessary to coin terminology for these processes, for customary terms such as "moralism" and "subjectivism" would risk troublesome ambiguities and also, very justly, the criticism of those who would be offended by the forced meaning of these terms. An additional advantage in the use of original terms lies in their capability of crystalizing and summing up the many nuances of the analyses presented.

[1] By *idea* or *notion* of God, the precise objective content of one's understanding of God is meant. The accent is on the intellectual element of the understanding. By *sense* of God, a relation of man with God in which the affectivity, the intellect and the will enter into play is meant, even though these powers are not explicitly specified. The *sense* of God involves a certain understanding, affective reaction and influence on practical conduct. These terms interact and their usage is a matter of stress. But the use of the term "sense" is an attempt to speak about the adolescent's relation with God as actually lived.

For each of these three over-all characteristics of the sense of God among adolescents, the problem will be proposed followed by a precise notion of the term and an analysis of its possible psychosociological motivations. A description of the Christian significance of each characteristic and some pedagogical orientations suggested by it will complete the discussion.

1. Naturation

1. *The Notion of Naturation.* By naturation[2] (of the sense of God or the religious sense) we mean a mentality[3] and expression in which God seems to be the term of man's efforts. Implied therein is a setting aside of the revelation of God given in Jesus Christ.

Naturation of the sense of God exists when the relationship with God appears to have no *definite* link with the God who has revealed himself in a Trinity of persons, or more often, when the relationship with God appears to be essentially motivated by natural experiences and needs. Such is the case, for example, when the notion of God the Father seems to be a transference of one's relationship with his parents.

---

[2] "Naturation" is a translation of the term *"naturalité"* which is commonly translated as "naturalization." However its usage here is coined by the author and it seemed best also to coin a corresponding English term which would guard the nominal and verbal sense, and which would also be less awkward—tr.

[3] Mentality: "Ensemble of intellectual dispositions, habits of the mind and fundamental beliefs of an individual" (Lalande, *Vocabulaire de Philosophie*).

This delicate notion seems to require further clarification.

a. *Naturation is not a pejorative term in this instance.*
It was precisely in order to avoid any pejorative nuance that the term "naturation" was coined. Such a nuance would have been almost inevitable if the term "naturalism" had been used.

b. *Expressing a concept of God in terms of natural understanding does not mean that this idea has not been learned as a result of revelation.*

When a young man writes: "God is the creator of the earth and the master of all," he could, in principle, have acquired this idea through the processes of reason alone. But does this mean that in fact he did so? The term "naturation" does not claim this. For such an idea could very well have been acquired as a result of revelation, for example through catechetical instruction, since in effect creation pertains to revelation.

c. *Naturation does not indicate the absence of all reference to revelation, but only the absence of reference to the specific elements of Christ's revelation.*

In positive terms, naturation means that the notion adolescents have of God does not explicitly express the God of Christ's revelation, that is, God the Father,[4] the Blessed Trinity, or God forming a covenant in Christ with all humanity.

However the term "naturation" excludes neither the revelation of creation as a personal act of God nor the

_____

[4] God the Father not in the sense of God the Creator, but in the sense of a fatherhood for all men in Christ and with Christ.

revelation of God's plan for the salvation of the world. In this area, adolescents look favorably on the Old Testament conception of God and its modern manifestations, for example, Negro spirituals.

d. *A natural understanding of God, in the sense of an understanding acquired through intelligent reflection on the created order, can in fact be lived in grace and influenced by grace.*

When an adolescent writes: "God is someone I need if I am to explain nature . . . He is a powerful and light breeze," it would not be possible to say that this natural understanding is not in fact mysteriously influenced by grace and implicitly impregnated with the whole life of the Church.

In conclusion, the term "naturation" indicates two basic notions:

—*the influence of natural tendencies:* the adolescent's understanding of God seems to be molded in part by heartfelt inclinations present in every man;

—*verbalization:* the adolescent's expression of his understanding of God has no explicit link with the historical order of revelation as revealed by Jesus Christ.

2. *Characteristics of Adolescent Naturation of the Sense of God.* The adolescent gives the impression that his sense of God is closer to natural religion than to historically revealed religion. Karl Rahner's comparison of the characteristics of the God of revelation with those of the God of theodicy will illustrate this point.

The acquisition of a sense of the God of revelation means first of all "liberating" all that is naturally true in other religions and philosophies and resituating these truths within the great organic unity of our creed.

Second, it means purifying ourselves of deviations in our concept of God which are the consequences of sin. It implies vigorously reacting against the tendency to utilize God, or bring him down to the level of our reasoning or of our sensitive perceptions: pantheism, idolatry, etc.

Finally, it means recalling that God manifested himself in the world by a sovereignly free action and that he freely calls man to enter into the intimacy of trinitarian communion.

The question is not whether or not adolescents actually live the grace of Christian faith. What is affirmed here is that adolescents do not have an explicit and conscious understanding of the God of historical revelation, in particular of God as revealed by Jesus Christ. Their sense or understanding of historical revelation is implicit and indefinite. The criteria set up by Karl Rahner[5] lead to the recognition that generally:

a. There is very little external evidence of an explicitly supernatural and revealed character in the adolescent's understanding of God. Adolescents tend to arrive at an understanding of God as a result of reason, education or natural needs. For example, they express themselves in this way: "God is a source of strength, of comfort in troublesome moments." Doubtless they use expressions similar to these of the Old Testament: "He is a landmark in torment, a guide over the heights, a refuge when I am lost . . ." But

[5] Karl Rahner, *Theological Investigations*, Baltimore 1959, vol. 1, 1–77. See especially, "The Prospects for Dogmatic Theology," 1–18.

the context indicates this is more a question of a God discovered through subjective need than of God recognized
in the light of faith.

b. Adolescents habitually bring God down to the level
of their feelings and tendencies, as is indicated by the following response: "God is someone I need in order to
explain nature. His presence fills me."

c. Lastly, adolescents rarely speak of the manifestation
of God's historical action calling man to enter into the new
covenant.

Thus, their language appears, in its external expression,
closer to the language of theodicy than to that of historical
revelation, especially that in which Jesus explains who his
Father is.

3. *Why There Is Religious Naturation.* Three causes
distinctly appear.

a. There is an assault by the instincts during adolescence. When Simone de Beauvoir describes her crisis of
faith in *Memoires of a Dutiful Daughter,* not once does
she speak of Jesus Christ. Did she know him other than as
a myth? This one example shows how much at this age,
in the expression of Paul Valery, the "gods in one's blood"
tend to submerge the reality of faith in the personal God
who spoke in history and who continues to touch men in
the Church. The god of the great cosmic forces tends to
eclipse the God revealed in Jesus Christ.

We cannot overstress the importance of instinctive factors in the religious behavior of the adolescent. Doctors and
psychologists have insisted repeatedly that from the ages
of 13 to 18 years instincts and drives are particularly force-

ful. And it is precisely this factor which provides the young person with a religion, or even a religious problematic, which seems more dependent on man's powerful natural tendencies than on the free intervention of God in history.

b. Another cause is no less decisive. It is the *naturalism or materialism of the ambient world* which continually degrades the original and specific character of Christian revelation. By natural inclination "this world" tends to annex revelation and deprive it of "its salt." Thus the faith of young people is continually corroded and assaulted by a multitude of worldly maxims, slogans, customs and illusions.

Think of the ideas on God and religion which modern means of communication can convey. Magazines, reviews, posters, films, radio and television result in the retention of only the exterior aspect, that coloring of religious truth which tickles the curiosity. For example, the imposing ceremonies of the Church are stressed, or curious phenomena relating more to natural religious feeling than to an authentic Christian life are highlighted. From the Bible some interesting stories may be cited or, at need, some well worn maxims retained which are nothing more than manifestations of good common sense or of philanthropic morality.

Finally, religion too often appears as man's own effort to link himself with, or if we may say it, to exploit the divinity, and not at all as God's personal call drawing men to a covenantal life with himself. As a result, Christianity is left only with natural elements and a rich foundation of pleasant stories which characterize a natural religion.

It has been frequently affirmed that man is not naturally supernatural. This assertion, which could be a tautology, indicates that God's intervention in the world does not necessarily affect man at the deepest level of his being. Man's natural development is so powerful that he tends to be content with himself, thus closing himself to the historical acts of God. Modern progress in science and technology accelerates this sense and desire for the human, and leads to a sort of natural religion.

In this milieu it is easy to understand the difficulty an adolescent would experience in accepting revelation, realizing its originality, and perceiving the way in which the gospel message abrogates the old dispensation. More likely he will confound Christianity and natural morality or place them on the same level.

c. A further distinction seems necessary. Catechesis and Christian education have not escaped corrosion by the idols of this world. A study of the reactions of young people and an analysis of their language leads to the conclusion that teaching and education have often been closer to a simple natural morality or theodicy than to the gospel and the doctrine of the Church.[6] In this regard, the way in which the adolescent was catechized as a child is of prime importance.

4. *The Value of This Stage.* A hypernaturation of the religious sense in adolescence can be spoken of. Does this

[6] A chaplain in a girls' school asked the pupils he had been preparing for a year for first communion what they thought of the catechism. After a moment's hesitation, one of them rose and asked: "Why do they ask in the catechism, 'What is God?' They should ask, 'Who is God?'"

natural prevalence have some positive signification? It does, and in two ways.

First, a sort of break in the form of religion the adolescent received rather spontaneously in his childhood is provoked by a violent eruption of instinctive forces and an accentuated sensitivity to natural realities. This is a beneficial experience which allows him to rethink religious truth and perhaps thus enter into a more personal faith.

Second, the life of faith until now characterized by familial or academic conditions will be enriched by the fervor and forms of these natural religious tendencies. The developing sense of the sacred will normally lead to a more urgent quest for God. Undoubtedly the sense of the sacred is not synonymous with faith. However, the impulse of natural desires opens man in a special way to a consciousness of transcendence.

In summary, this stage of adolescent preoccupation with natural reality is a privileged period in the development of religious consciousness. Certainly it is a dangerous period with its risks of deviation and imprisonment. But it is also a period rich in its drives, in the force and quality of its opening toward something greater than man.

5. *The Providential Character of Naturation.* Advances in the study of religious psychology, particularly in its genetic aspect, lead to a fundamental hypothesis. This hypothesis constitutes a sort of key to the interpretations proposed here.

It seems that every man, for his own benefit, is called to pass through the great stages of salvation history. From the beginning a child possesses everything in seed, and the stages of human maturation are providential occasions for becoming more conscious of this seed, for broadening and correcting what is already present. Childhood is open to an understanding of creation and the moral life of the law. Adolescence is open to the Old Testament, especially to an understanding of the presence and friendship of Christ, and adulthood is open to Pentecost and a life according to the Spirit.

From this perspective it would be incongruous to criticize the naturation of adolescents. Adolescence is a privileged religious period, animated by the Spirit, leading toward a fuller understanding of the true God. Before rediscovering Christ, like Peter after Pentecost, the adolescent must first of all discover him in the mysterious progress of the Exodus and in Pharisaic zeal, in the despairs of the desert and in the joys of the promised land.

If man received the whole revelation of the God of Jesus Christ at once, what would become of human freedom? And from God's point of view, what would become of the incarnation—God's progressive entrance into the world of man? The little child must proceed through his parents' understanding of God before personally and consciously knowing the God of Jesus Christ. The 10 to 12-year-old child must pass through the God of objective instruction. The adolescent must rise above an understanding of God impregnated with subjective tendencies. As for the adult, following the light of Pentecost he will begin to discern the God of Jesus Christ as he is encountered in the "objective Church," in the events and reality of life.

In conclusion, if the prophet denounces a certain deism

in adolescents, the educator knows that there is a providential state involved. Certainly it must be surpassed and purified, but it must also be respected as the manifestation of a plan of God's wisdom for man.

6. *Naturation and Education.* In this section one aspect of the problem will be highlighted: the risk the teacher of adolescents runs in presenting the faith solely in a rational and systematic form. The most tragic result would be to be unfaithful to the Christian message itself. A completely rational presentation of the faith would probably give the impression that revelation is subordinated to reason and that the historical intervention of God in the world is merely a natural development of human striving. This is the risk present in a certain theology where, in fact, the faith appears to young people as a philosophical superstructure.[7]

In order to assure proper education in the case of naturation, it is important at certain times that *catechesis break* with adolescent ways of thinking and that it carefully distinguish the calls of man from the personal intervention of God.

This study indicates that, in order to accede to the order of historical revelation, it is important to note another adolescent need. It is not only necessary carefully to distinguish historical revelation from the natural pursuit of God, but also to address adolescents in modes of expres-

[7] To hear a large number of adults speak, the catechesis they received based on manuals such as *The Baltimore Catechism* has not been able to avoid this stumbling block.

sion and *categories of thought adapted to their unique age-levels.*

It has already been noted that preadolescents who responded to the inquiry were voluntarily dependent on an academic framework, precise formulas, or rational systems. With pubescent adolescents, on the contrary, the natural categories of reason were eclipsed by the natural categories of the heart and feelings. Now, on this level, it appeared that their faith was no longer sufficiently clarified by the academic bases of their catechism. These bases no longer affected them. Catechesis had not given them forms susceptible, at the proper moment, of really touching and christianizing their natural religious sense with love. Perhaps the language of catechesis has been adapted to children, but as yet catechetical language has not been adapted to adolescents.

It seems evident that it is necessary to give children from 10 to 12 years of age a system of objective formulas and frameworks of thought. Some of the responses received from preadolescents have shown the advantage of this approach. But to be content with this approach would result in a grave shortcoming, especially for adolescents whose mental structure is open to other approaches.

A limited study of adolescents in a Protestant milieu was also undertaken. From this and also from the results furnished by several Catholic schools, we come to see more fully the task that is before us. Adolescents are responsive to biblical and liturgical modes of thought since these are filled with symbolism, with the dimensions of interpersonal relationships, and with historical and dynamic, and not simply static and abstract perspectives. This is a language adolescents understand.

If the adolescent's sense of God seems more romantic and natural than Christian, this is perhaps because teachers have not been able to reach him on his own ground. Rather their language has been almost unilaterally fixed in the categories of adults, or of "second childhood."

Finally, this study has shown that in late adolescence and young adulthood (and day-to-day experience proves this), young people require a synthesis and an apologetic which are not only expressed in terms of reason, nature and being. They demand first of all a terminology of the heart, of person and of action.

When a rational presentation of catechesis is combined with one that is more symbolic, inductive and existential, the catechesis is still presented on a natural plane. No single mode of presentation conveys in itself the revelation of Jesus Christ. But it is important to emphasize that naturation of the Christian message is due in part to its rational and systematic presentation. It is not a question of choosing between a rational presentation and an historical or existential presentation. Rather these modes of presentation should be mixed, and it should be noted that the mental structure of adolescents is less in accord with rational systematization.

2. Egomorphism

Egomorphism is the second characteristic of the religious sense of adolescents. What does this term mean? Rather

than define it immediately, it might be well for us briefly
to note the progress of our research vis-á-vis the responses
to the inquiry.

A reading of the responses soon revealed that the idea
and sense of God expressed by adolescents were greatly
marked with the personality of the individual. This was
so much the case that one member of the research team
remarked that there are as many gods as young people!
Spontaneously a word suggested itself: adolescents are "sub-
jectives."

But what could be meant by the subjectivity or subjectivism of adolescents? Would it mean that in perceiving
the divine reality the adolescent deformed it or repressed
certain of its essential characteristics, thereby transforming
it to his own desires? Would it mean that the adolescent
was profoundly and affectively involved in his act of understanding, just as a mother in her subjective understanding
of her child? Such concepts, true as they are, seemed in-
sufficient and vague.

Having thus caught a glimpse of the general direction
of the inquiry, we proceeded to scrutinize more closely the
adolescents' responses. In what way, we asked, were these
statements subjective? What would characterize the subjectivity or subjectivism of such statements? In "reëvaluat-
ing" the responses, a more precise characteristic gradually
came to the fore, a characteristic we designated by the term
"egomorphism."

The meaning of egomorphism can now be more clearly
specified. However, before rendering an interpretation, we

must first attempt to discern the adolescent forms and motivations of egomorphism.

THE CONTENT OF EGOMORPHISM

1. *The Data.* In what, we might ask, does the egomorphism of the adolescent's religious sense consist? This question can be considered from the perspective of the different age groups and their points of view. The frequency of certain words is inversely related percentagewise in preadolescence and late adolescence. When this inverse percentage is very marked, it always involves words characterizing either a very objective or a very subjective concept of God.

In this regard, the most typical words for characterizing God are those of "Spirit" (objective concept), and "confidant" or "friend" (subjective concept). The percentages are:

	Preadolescence	Pubescent Adolescence	Late Adolescence
Spirit	32.5	21.3	14.5
Confidant-Friend	4.	12.	13.

The inversion of percentages is immediately apparent. The more one approaches adolescence, the more he leaves catechetical and objective formulas behind, now depicting God according to his feelings and the needs of his age.

Even more characteristic is the consideration of the different *points of view between boys and girls.* Could there be a God of boys and a God of girls? These points should be noted:

The notion of pure divine spirituality is never marked among girls, while it appears very frequently among boys. For example, a boy argues thus: "God is a pure spirit, without a body, thus immortal. In the beginning, everything is pure spirit; with a body, spirit becomes more or less a slave. Purity is the model of all virtues." Or: "God is a loving and pure spirit . . ."

The notion of a faithful and good God to the point of making him a confidant is typically feminine. Girls will say: "God is a Father who desires my happiness." "My protector . . . my refuge . . . my confidant." "A Father who helps me." But among boys the notion of an *ideal* God, the giver of graces for the *moral combat*, is clearly apparent. "God is the leader, the guide." "A light I ought to attain." "The great leader who has all perfections."

These examples illustrate the influence of sexual conditioning in adolescents.

Finally, in addition to the effects of age and sex, the absolutely unique and *personal* note found in each of the responses, especially as we near late adolescence, should be mentioned. The influence of the character of each person is so great that it is extremely difficult to assemble so many nuances into a few general categories.

2. *General Statements.* The dominance of subjectivity in the religious sense of adolescents made apparent by the investigation leads to the following general observations:

a. *As young adulthood is approached, the responses become more subjective* in the good sense of the word, that is, in the sense that the subject's affective spontaneity, affective choices and will-reactions are involved in his un-

derstanding of God. His responses also become more subjective in the pejorative sense of the word, that is, in the
sense that the subject's notion of God is dependent on his
own interior demands and the nuances of his age and
temperament. At the most extreme point, God is brought
down to the dimensions of adolescent needs.

b. *As a temperament is more affective, subjective factors are more likely to be present and play a more determin-
ing role* in the understanding of God. This much could
have been suspected from simple psychological deduction.
But it is good to note that the data confirm this conclusion.
Let us look at some percentages for the notion of God as
confidant.

	Boys	Girls
Preadolescence	2.65	5.3
Pubescent Adolescence	8.65	15.3
Late Adolescence	7.	18.65

God as confidant appears more readily and forcefully
among more affective girls. In addition to this general data,
and beyond the generally more pronounced characteristic
of affectivity among girls, an analysis of each of the responses, and particularly the responses to the other questions of the inquiry, directs attention to the affective
dominant and its consequences for the adolescent's meaning of God. The girl desires God to be a solid, faithful and
present support, fulfilling her affective needs. Her need for
God resembles her need for a father and an ideal man.

Affective adolescents tend to believe in God only insofar

as they sense him. They also tend to imagine God according to their particular feelings at the moment.

But not everything is negative among adolescents. They tend more than others to interiorize the notion of God. They rapidly and profoundly assimilate the instruction they receive, assuming it into a personal synthesis enhanced by the riches of their own personality. And more than others, they are open to the mystery of the covenant and a living, rich and spontaneous dialogue with the God of Jesus Christ.

c. When a mentality is more dominated by reason, subjective factors tend to appear later, or more weakly. This is particularly true of preadolescents and the boys among them, especially those who are less spontaneous because of objective and rational demands. (This was found to be especially true in certain French technical schools and in several industrial sectors.)

Such a person is more attentive to the objective nature of what he is taught and the demands of society. If there is any subjective coloring in his notion of God it will be in his sense of God's solidity and rationality.

d. A generalized doubting, a crisis of faith, becomes more likely (as young adulthood is approached) when the adolescent's intelligence is more active and his emotions more violent and dominated by his imagination. This results, on the one hand, from a confrontation between the God spontaneously received in childhood and the God imposed by sociological conditions, and subjective demands on the other. This conclusion (which seems very important to us) became clear from the study of the responses of late adolescents.

Forceful emotions and a lively intelligence have already been mentioned. By these terms the individual character-istics pertaining to the character of each person are indi-cated. But there is more. It could be added that the sociological factor enters into play, rousing the imagination and more or less violently jostling the sensitivity of the adolescent. Thus it is clear that the very liberal education of certain public schools, with the frequent proposition therein of new and more or less subversive theories to adolescents, plays the role of a stimulus to their imagina-tion and disposes them to question the faith.

3. *The Notion of Egomorphism.* What can be con-cluded from these general statements about the influence of subjectivity on the adolescent's understanding of God? Essentially we can list only two main conclusions:

a. Subjective factors profoundly influence the adoles-cent's understanding of God.

b. Subjective factors influence the sense of God in two ways. On the one hand, they distort divine reality with the forms and demands of adolescent subjectivity; on the other hand, they greatly involve the adolescent's personal-ity in his understanding of God.

These two ways are more or less proportioned to age, sex and character. To condense them into the single term "subjectivism" or even "subjectivity" would seem to be a grave imprecision, if not a misunderstanding. Therefore, the term "egomorphism" was preferred over these ambiguous terms. This term could draw our study toward its essential concept: *God, during adolescence, tends to be given the form of the ego.* It would also avoid the pejorative nuances of the term "subjectivism" and the too restricted meaning of "subjectivity."

We are now able to propose the following *definition of religious egomorphism:* religious egomorphism is a mentality[8] and form of expression in which one's concept of God or relationship with God seems profoundly determined by the psychosociological conditions of the subject's personality.

IMPORTANT ADOLESCENT FORMS OF EGOMORPHISM

Egomorphism can appear in many forms, from fetishism to sentimentalism. In order better to characterize adolescent egomorphism, we shall discuss two of its more prominent forms, namely pseudo-pantheism and idealization.

1. *Pseudo-pantheism.* Like Mendousse and many other psychologists, we noticed a certain pantheism among adolescents. But, this pantheism must be precisely defined. There is no question here of a philosophical doctrine in which God and the world are one in a continuity of nature. Rather this is a case of a particular sensitivity to God's relationship with the world which does not consider his transcendence. Thus one could speak, with more truth, of an immanentism of God caused by an accentuated symbolic sense. The adolescent is at an age when he senses

_____

[8] See no. 3 above, the notion of mentality.

"universal correspondences," the intercommunication of different levels of being. This is why he expresses himself in such ambiguous expressions as: "To me God seems present in all that I see, in nature, the universe, in everything." "We sense his presence in nature."

Simone de Beauvoir succinctly describes this symbolic sense of the God of nature: "Much more keenly than in Paris I sensed the presence of God around me. In Paris, men and their buildings hid him from me. Here I could see the plants and the clouds just as he had brought them out of chaos, and they bore his mark. The more attached I became to the earth, the nearer I came to him, and each walk was an act of adoration. His sovereignty did not take mine away. He knew all things in his way, that is, absolutely, but it seemed to me that, in a certain way, he needed my eyes if the trees were to have color. How could a pure spirit have tested the heat of the sun, and the freshness of the dew, without my body? . . . Each morning when I leaped over the white railings to plunge into the forest, it was he who called me. With complacency he watched me survey the world he had created for me to see . . ."[9]

The perception of relationships, of the interior links between God, beings and things is the characteristic of the symbolic sense. By means of this sense a person sees the

[9] Simone de Beauvoir, *Memoires of a Dutiful Daughter*, Cleveland 1959, 123. It is certain that this romantic sense of the God of nature is actually outmoded. But it is the material reality of the symbol which has changed, and not the symbolic reality itself. Certain young people, who no longer see God in a rushing stream, perceive him in the power of a dam and its machinery, a work or man.

relationship between material and spiritual realities, between himself and things.

The symbolic language evident throughout the responses of young people from 15 to 18 years of age corresponds to this accentuated symbolic sense. It is an extremely imprecise language, but one suggestive and full of an imagery of archetypes, reveries, poetry, flights, gestures and attitudes.

The Symbolic Sense of Adolescents

Why does this emergence, this hyperactivity of the symbolic sense of adolescents, occur?

Symbol essentially means relationship. But the relationship of material realities to spiritual realities occurs through man's mediation. Again, the relationship of the spiritual to the material is the stronger insofar as man is a better point of contact, the point of union of matter and spirit. The very etymological meaning of the word "symbol" is found here (*symballein*, fr. Gr., to put together, to compare two sides).

The following diagram illustrates this concept:

Matter $\longleftrightarrow$ Man $\longleftrightarrow$ Spirit
(Things)   (God)

In and through symbol, man takes these two extremes with and into himself.

It could even be said that at that moment when man is most related to matter and to spirit, he will have the strongest symbolic sense.

Now, is adolescence not one of those privileged times

when man is linked (as much by temperament as by existential situation) to both matter and spirit?[10]

It is especially through his instincts insofar as they are biological that man is strongly related to the animal kingdom and to the material world. And who, more than the adolescent, is influenced by instincts to the point of being almost completely submerged by biological pressures and ruled by sensible perceptions?[11] Around the age of 15 the young person frequently experiences a sort of "dissolution" of his being in physical sensations. Metaphorically this experience could be likened to the influence of a salt water bath, a ski slope, or the first days of spring![12] As a result of this "plunge into nature" through the instincts, a sort of symbolic hyperactivity is realized, that is, a highly accentuated sense of affinity with the universe, of intercommunication between the levels of being.

One could say that the adolescent communes with the world soul. Wallon uses the word "participation" to ex-

[10] We could also speak, perhaps on other grounds, of childhood and old age.

[11] One could say as much, and for the same reasons, of primitive peoples, of every person or of every historical period when instincts are unleashed. Thus, in their beginnings, all great revolutionary movements are full of mythical symbols and images which will be toned down in a more rationalized stage.

[12] Romanticism, like the symbolism of Baudelaire or Rimbaud, expresses this reality well:

Mais la nature est là qui t'invite et qui t'aime,
Plonge-toi dans son sein qu'elle t'ouvre toujours.
                                          Lamartine

The adolescent, especially at certain times, seems immersed in what is material, by his instinctive powers, like a sponge in the ocean. He has a more or less clear, but forceful consciousness of the "circulation of unheard of vigor" and he is vivified.

press a similar phenomenon in early childhood. The adolescent is conscious in a confused sort of way that things participate in each other through a kind of consubstantiality.[13]

On the other hand, one might say that the adolescent experiences a strong pull toward spiritual entities, toward the absolute, toward what psychoanalysts call "decarnalization." We shall return to this aspect later.

Since adolescence is an age in which the attractions of the material and the spiritual are so strongly experienced, it is not surprising that the adolescent is particularly sensitive to symbol. Although this concept can only be mentioned briefly here, it undoubtedly merits more development, for it is an important key to an understanding of adolescent psychology.

2. *Idealization.* Idealization is another major form of adolescent egomorphism. Here the adolescent interprets the absolute in terms of his own ego and thus subconsciously modifies the Divinity. God for the adolescent, writes Jean Lacroix, "is the adolescent purified, sublimated."[14]

Idealization is a process in which the individual tends to forget God's historical and objective characteristics in order to confer on him an imaginary reality based on the thrust of subjective tendencies of the personality toward the absolute.

That this process leads to a modified notion of God is only normal. It is even a necessary process in all human

[13] This word was first used by Lévy-Bruhl to characterize the primitive mentality.

[14] J. Lacroix, *Timidité et Adolescence,* 128.

understanding of God. But because this idealization often obscures the historical and objective divine characteristics and sometimes mistakes idealized subjective realities for the divine reality, adolescent idealization often takes on a pejorative aspect.

The data of the inquiry aid in an understanding of this mentality.

How Boys and Girls Idealize God

The phenomenon of idealization of God could be studied in the light of different periods of adolescence or in the light of different environments. Here, however, the emphasis will be more on the physical and psychological differences between boys and girls.

Two typical expressions, which have already been mentioned, will exemplify the responses. The first is by a boy, the second by a girl:

"God is a pure spirit, without a body . . . In the beginning everything is pure spirit; with a body, spirit becomes . . . a slave. Purity is the model of all the virtues."

"God is almost the only one who understands me well, but I often forget him . . . I would like to love and be loved not with an invisible love like that of God, but with a human love whom I can see, sense, and to whom I can give myself."

How far away and inaccessible God is in both these cases! However the two cases are different. The boy idealizes God by depriving him of historical significance, or personal reality, and above all of affective "human-divine" interpersonal relationship. God becomes a vanishing point at the horizon and the young adolescent wears himself out running toward it. Is this a case of absolutization of the ego, or Narcissus dreaming of his ideal image? There are elements of this, but the relationship is not entirely negative.

If, in relation to God, the boy seems to idealize his "I alone," the girl, on the contrary, tends to idealize her relation to a man. This is why the notion of "God the confidant" is characteristic of female psychology. The boy sees in God a point to attain; the girl sees a relationship to realize. Each point of view is very different. But we should not be deceived, for the process is the same. Though more rational for the boy and more affective for the girl, the concept of God is no less a certain creation of the individual, based on an "absolutization" of the needs of the ego.

Any exaggeration of these points would lead to falsehood. But it is necessary objectively to diagnose this spontaneous psychological process in which the historical and revealed characteristics of God are, so to speak, set to one side. This process results in a certain invention of a divinity ruled by temperamental and compensatory needs.

WHY ADOLESCENTS IDEALIZE GOD

A 17-year-old boy, a student at a public high school, said that he would get up at night, open the dormitory window, and contemplate the stars. "I think of the girl I love," he said. "She is a star." Psychologists, analyzing the affective evolution of man, stress that between the ages of 13 and 18 years, love attains a maximum of "decarnalization." That is to say, it is at this time that the greatest separation between love as a spiritual relation and love as a physical reality exists. And is this not the age of such strong oscillations between the spirit and the flesh? Is this not the age when a boy sometimes even writes letter to a girl he has never met?

It seems that the adolescent idealizes God for the same reasons that he idealizes his friend or, in a more general way, every object he encounters whether it concerns life, the future or friendship.

What are the reasons? Why this spontaneous process of idealization? Three very important and versatile principles will now be analyzed. These principles we could have analyzed anywhere in this book, however, for they explain not only idealization, but the whole of adolescent religious behavior.

1. *Idealization and the Internal Need for Self-Realization.* By definition an adolescent is a being in quest of his own personality, a being who is striving to become. As he grows his dependence on his parents is lessened and his sights are set toward the future. He wishes to be "a worthwhile person" and to make a success of his life. He wishes to develop all the riches of the talents and powers he is astonished to discover in himself.

The adolescent's drive toward something *beyond himself* is powerfully fueled by the interior turmoil which draws him away from the comfortable situations of his childhood and gives his objectives an aura of fervor. Me-

diocrity is intolerable to the adolescent. For him an ideal
becomes "the ideal." Truth, justice and love become great
causes meriting resounding and revolutionary actions.

How could God escape this universal sonorization. In
line with this drive toward an ideal I, the adolescent tends
subconsciously to conceive God as the absolute of his ego.

Will he remember what he has been taught of the revealed God and what the Church says of God each day?
Doubtless he will remember less than he does at other
ages. Under the pressure of exploding instincts, imagination
supersedes perception. Sensitivity to objective realities is
diminished by the subjective drives which dominate him.
This form of idealization is based on the ego, although in
some places today the process of idealization may take on
mutated forms.

In his psychosociological analyses, Riesman[15] has shown
the importance of the three great sociocultural groups
which influence idealization. For tradition-directed societies (group 1), the ideal is a reproduction of the norms imposed by the tradition of ancestors, by the founders of the
country. For culturally varied societies (group 2, inner-
directed)—this was the case with many European cities at
the beginning of the century—the ideal, indelibly instilled
in the child's psyche by parents and their substitutes, consists in being faithful to a rather tyrannical "superego." In
this line a whole generation tried to succeed individually
in a bad sense by trying to satisfy a subconscious ideal
ineradicably inculcated in them through education. The

[15] David Riesman, M. Glazer, R. Denney, *The Lonely Crowd,*
2nd ed. New Haven 1953.

young people reached in our study, particularly those from parochial schools, belonged in general to this sociocultural group. For them God appeared as a parental superego, and idealization was based on this superego.

Today young people belong more to another sociocultural group, a group which sociologists have called "radar" in distinction to group 2, called, aptly enough, "gyroscope" —the term "gyroscope" implying that the group is fixedly oriented toward an immutable interior pole, whatever the environment. The radar group (group 3, other-directed) is not determined by the internal factors of a tyrannical superego, since this superego has not been inculcated by our modern hesitant and unsettled education. Rather this group is essentially determined by a need to be like the group. What counts for the other-directed group is neither ideology nor the teacher nor the crystallized hero of the superego, but *being together*, being in harmony with the thought, norms and action of the group. Successful magazines such as *Seventeen* are typical of this mentality. What is there here of an internal demand for self-realizing idealization?

The present study did not adequately answer this question. It is clear, however, that this mentality occurs especially among young people in public schools, where the parental superego is less forceful. From experience it seems that this new form of idealization can be characterized as follows: yesterday it was the parents who were the source of the superego, of the ideal pursued, and thus of the form in which God was idealized. Today it is *the group*. Young people no longer base their idealization on their parental superego, but *on what is better in the group, in their environment*. Thus God is now being identified more with the soul and norm of the group. As a group ideal, God is presence, certitude, strength, value, quality and exigence.

2. *Idealization as Compensation for Dissatisfaction*. The more human beings experience an emptiness the more they search for a complement or fulfillment. "Depth calls on depth," says the Bible. Because he desires to become, the adolescent is timid and dissatisfied. His normal tendency is to compensate for this emptiness and interior suffering with a sort of artificial nourishment produced in his imagination, which will pacify him or even gratify him in an illusory way. This is well known by those publishers who weekly feed young girls material for their ideal-love dream. How could God, who is "everything man could desire," escape this more or less conscious process of affective compensation? The tendency is so strong that adolescents do not realize the naivete of their words. "I pray to God . . . because my love for my parents must be poured out to someone," one young student wrote.

3. *Idealization as Evasion in Face of the Personal Experience of Life*. Until now the adolescent had been protected by his parents and the whole milieu of his childhood. Now, rather brusquely around the age of 11 to 15 years, powerful sensations bring insecurity. The world frequently seems to be a hostile reality threatening him for his weakness and struggle for personality. Parents and adults are not the models he formerly believed them to be.

"I had a strange experience," writes a 17-year-old student. "I wanted to find a job for a young girl, at whatever price

. . . but all my impatience, vigor and confidence ran up against the indifference of officials who didn't give a damn. I touched life. I didn't know it."

Faced with the harshness of life and the discovery of the necessity of adaptation to reality, the adolescent often reacts by escaping in one of two ways.

The first of these is to escape into a world of his own making. Piaget in particular has studied this aspect of adolescent thought,[16] and his studies could be applied to an understanding of God. Not being strong enough to accept the world as it is and the revealed God as he reveals himself, the adolescent imagines or recreates them on his own terms. He sets up a hypothetical God to which he submits God himself. Who has not heard the passionate adolescent's charges of God's injustice? And what do they really mean if not this: "If God were exactly like me he would have made the world differently."[17] Here we see how his thought "creates" God by denying reality's dependence on the creator. This mechanism would be the mortal sin par excellence if it were not subconscious!

The other manner of escape is the *return to a secure and idealized past*. The adolescent nostalgically approaches God as if he were a lost paradise of childhood and his mother.

The adolescent, between the ages of 12 and 16, has just broken with the familiar universe of his childhood. Why

---

[16] B. Inhelder and J. Piaget, *The Growth of Logical Thinking from Childhood to Adolescence*, New York 1958.

[17] The adolescent is startled when he is asked to show—based on facts (e.g. the Bible)—where God reveals himself as unjust and wicked.

would he not tend to regret the loss of this secure and protected world and to confer on it a paradisaic character touching the absolute. In most parts of Europe and America people want first communions to be held before the age of 12 because, they say, before this age children are "innocent" and "we can have a beautiful celebration for pure souls." This is a very symptomatic conception. Purity equals innocence,[18] the absence of trouble, and finally the absence of agitation and rebellion in this case. Purity means being preserved within a closed universe. After the age of 12 the child will enter the world and may dirty his hands.

We have previously studied the concept of purity among boys from ages 12 to 16. These studies have shown almost without exception that none of them speaks in positive terms of love. Purity is essentially "not doing." In this manner of seeing things there is an attempt to return to idealized childhood. Purity is returning to the lost world of childhood. Purity is not having trouble with the body. At its most extreme, purity is not entering the world.[19] The already cited response of a boy summarizes the attitude: "In the beginning [childhood] everything is pure spirit. With a body, spirit becomes a slave."

Who, then, is God? Essentially God is one who has not soiled himself with the body and the world, he who has kept his original spirituality, the "pure spirit." And, as a

[18] With a slightly pejorative nuance: "He is so innocent!"
[19] Is not the success of the The Little Prince by Saint-Exupéry linked in part to this mentality?

consequence, God is he to whom one must *return* (a return to the past). That there are elements of truth in such conceptions is evident. But we must learn to measure the danger of being satisfied with such primitive and unpurified forms of sensitivity and understanding. Have not parents and teachers unconsciously added to the problem by exaggeratedly exalting the beautiful models of wise children, picturing them as children without virility or creative freedom.[20]

SIGNIFICANCE OF ADOLESCENT EGOMORPHISM

The Passage from the Immanent to the Incarnate God. Bremond recounts the story of a young man who confided his doubts and the crisis of his religious faith to an old priest. The priest said to him: "My friend, the problem is that you have not yet found your God." Here the accent should be placed on the possessive "your." The young person must find *his* God if he desires to live and not stifle in religion.

The significance of adolescent egomorphism is that it calls the young person to interiorize, personally to assume the objective notion of God conveyed to him during his childhood, and too spontaneously and perhaps too abstractly adhered to until now.

From the labyrinth of egomorphism the young person should make the following discovery: God is not an In-

[20] Is there an influence of bourgeois ideas here? See those pictures of first communion where idealization continues, those holycards of boys and girls dressed in purest white and radiating holiness.

Self hidden behind the stars. He is not a potentate, or someone indifferent to "me." He is a living person who speaks to me now and invites me to fulfill my desire to live in a divine way, in Jesus Christ. This is called *the personal discovery of the mystery of the incarnation.*

This seems to be the important significance of egomorphism. This is the true "sense of history" on the adolescent level. An accentuated symbolic sense, immanentism, idealization, pseudo-pantheism: all these mechanisms, which tend to bring God down to man's level in an idolatrous act of appropriation, can also serve to open man to the God who calls him to a sacred covenant.

But how can egomorphism lead to such a discovery? As we have shown, the adolescent tends to reject a God who is not related to him. If his reason finds value in such a God, his heart protests. His thirst to live fully and in the absolute is such that he prefers to shrink God to his own dimensions or idealize himself to God's dimensions, rather than believe in a God who would not make his life secure, or who would not answer the demands of his heart and soul. Undoubtedly any process which brings God down to one's level is untenable. But the subjective need which underlies it, that is, the need for a God who would be *absolutely God* while at the same time *near like a friend*, seems to be the best road toward an understanding and acceptance of the incarnate God. For this the adolescent need only go beyond a God who would be a friend or essential absolute because of subjective needs, to a God who is a friend because of his infinite mercy. This is Jesus Christ.

THE RISKS OF ENGULFMENT AND DEVIATION

Some people will insist that each man must be completely converted. And how can anyone contest this? One would have to be very naive not to realize the danger the adolescent runs of never surpassing a more or less romanticized and subjectivized God of nature.

The Christian reader may experience some uneasiness in realizing the extent to which an adolescent, in all candor, is capable of inventing God. One is reminded here of the impassioned reaction of the prophets of the Old Testament to all forms of idolatry. Once man prostrated himself before the golden calf. To modern man this seems gross and inexcusable. But does not the adolescent—and, in general, modern man—fall into an analogous idolatry?

Although more subtle than adoring a golden calf, is it not in the same idolatrous vein to serve an ideal self-image or to deck God out in the vestments of one's own subjectivity? Is this not divinization of an element of creation? Is this not fabricating an image of God? The prophets said to the people: "Be converted to God with your whole heart, and rid yourselves of the strange gods in your midst . . ." Should not modern man also listen to these words? Today perhaps one could easily transpose this statement from the sociological to the psychological level: "Remove from your depths, from your psyche, the false ideal god you have raised, this ego to whom you consecrate your life, and be converted to the true God"!

When the adolescent is caught up in the formation of his

personality, when the pressure of instincts drives him, the danger is great that he will remain a prisoner of his ego and listen to the tumultuous voice of his nature to such an extent that he will become incapable of being a "hearer of the word"! The teacher should not forget that educating consists of both understanding and depending on these stages, and in reacting to them.

EDUCATION AND EGOMORPHISM

Two important approaches can be suggested which might lead to a total education.

1. *With the Tendency toward Egomorphism as a Basis, the Teacher Should Develop a Sense of the Incarnation in His Students.* The first step in this direction is to help the adolescent recognize the presence and action of God in his life, feelings and reactions. Tresmontant stresses the fact that God revealed himself to his people in the Old Testament through "historical demonstration." This was a process by which a prophet enlightened the collective, historical experience of the people.[21] With the aid of a prophet and by interpreting their own history, the people became conscious of the presence and action of Yahweh. Thus they discovered how God intervened in their history. The modern adolescent is not so susceptible to this historical reading. The presence and action of God in the Christian people, in the Church, leave him cold. On the

[21] C. Tresmontant, *Toward the Knowledge of God*, Baltimore 1961.

other hand, he is quite open to the discovery of God within his personal life and even within the world.

At this age it is essential to reveal the God of Jesus Christ, as much through a reform of life as through a catechesis which prophesies about life. This is not a God "alone and above," but a God within realities. The adolescent will only personally be touched by the God of Jesus Christ when he discovers God in the covenant he makes with him today, in the events of his personal life and that of the group. Thus the Magdalene recognized Jesus Christ at the tomb only at the moment when she experienced him as someone calling her by name: Myriam.[22]

2. *The Deviations of Naturalism, Intimatism and Subjectivism Must Be Reacted against.* Freud, Marx and Sartre, each in his own manner, have reproached religion for being nothing but the transference of man's needs to the absolute. It is easy to say that in thus attacking religion they only attacked caricatures of God. But in fact these caricatures are founded on something real, on a multitude of believers who are still infants or adolescents in the faith.

[22] If God had not become incarnate, mankind would have little way of knowing him. But in Jesus Christ it is revealed that God is known through his sharing in our name and our human history.

In other words, it is not in explaining the archetypes of his subconscious, the conclusions of his reason, or the fruit of his natural observations that man knows the God of Jesus Christ, but in progressively accepting the measures by which God historically enters into man's life. As a man grows he knows the God of Jesus Christ insofar as he is conscious that God loves him, calls him by his name, and confides a task to him.

The teacher must vigorously demythologize these adolescent "subjectivizations" of God. He must act prudently and at the appropriate time lest he risk killing the seeds of a good evolution by too brusquely uprooting the weeds of deviation. However it is sometimes best to speak forcefully, whether to make a sort of *prophetic proclamation of the true God* in the face of caricatures,[23] or more often in order to provoke the adolescent's conscience to a realization of how he fabricates caricatures of God because of his unsatisfied needs.

Faced with egomorphism, the teacher must try to prevent the adolescent from lingering or wasting away in a childish religion. He must prevent the adolescent from being content with a too subjective or inconsistent behavior and try to lead his intense personal search to an understanding of the mystery of the incarnation. For egomorphism seems to be the dominant characteristic of the sense of God among adolescents.

[23] For this reason we must unmask the myth of God whose absolute spirituality is conceived a little too much like a snowy summit and not like merciful charity: a God whose spirituality would consist in not entering into the world, in not encountering man as body and flesh! Moreover, to illustrate the true visage of God, catechetical statements will not suffice. An adolescent sees God in those who surround him. He "appraises" God through the values proposed by his teachers.

In both the schools and the family, it would be good on this subject not only to extol the values of order, regularity and passive submission, but also and even more so, to extol the values of charity in action. Without doubt the necessities of common life at home and at school demand a framework and a discipline. But this should not exhaust the meaning of God the Father! Let the God of Jesus Christ be shown especially in the creative action of charity, humble attention to others, service even to the cross, love for the oppressed, and in generous and disinterested pardon.

NOTE

On the Structural Differences in the Apprehension of God between Boys and Girls

This study indicated that boys and girls perceive God in different ways. There are two forms of egomorphism, based on the respective psychologies of the boy and of the girl. How can they be characterized?

Two key phrases characterize the feminine mode of apprehension: sensitivity to person-to-person relationships, and sensitivity to the individual, existential aspect of realities (with a dominance of intuition). The phrases "sensitivity to action" and "sensitivity to the general and universal aspect of things" (with a dominance of the rational) characterize the masculine mode of apprehension. Let us clarify this distinction.

FEMININE PSYCHOLOGY

The religious universe of the girl seems to be organized around a person-to-person relationship with God. Very dependent on nature and quite open to people and tradition, the girl does not so much seek in religion a logical and coherent system which would permit her to dominate the world and impose her law on history. Rather she seeks *harmony* in dependence, a support and *stabilizing accord* in her relationship with God. Her feminine need is not so much to dominate nature (as is the case with men), as it is to live and give life.

The responses received from girls verified this relational organization of their religion. The dynamic principle of their religious synthesis is an *individual relationship with a divine Person*. It is on this level that choices are made and drives fed. Crises were even stirred up because "we do not sense God"! Girls will say, for example: "God is a person of love, very near to me . . . the true goal of my life" (an 18-year-old girl). But on the other hand, there is crisis: "I would like to love and be loved, but not with an invisible love like God's, but with a human love you can see, one you can *sense* and to whom you can give yourself."

Because of its consequences, especially on the level of religious instruction, it is very necessary to stress the importance of this relational need. A synthesis must always be organized around a principle, a sort of axis in virtue of which we distinguish, compare and unite the elements of a whole. If the principle around which the synthesis is constructed does not correspond to the mental structure of an individual, this person, instead of entering profoundly into the synthesis, submits to it exteriorly. The proposed synthesis will, therefore, always be a framework learned by rote, an accidental reference, rather than a doctrine of thought and life. Is this not what happens when fine logical syntheses organized around a static exploration of dogma in terms of nature and substance are proposed to girls?

Undoubtedly such syntheses have value and are necessary, especially on the scientific level.[24] But we should note

---

[24] Doubtless it may be necessary in catechesis to convey precise notions through reference to the categories of substance. Here we wish to speak only of the synthesis and dynamic principle which underlie them.

that they are generally inept for transmitting a living Christianity.

The situation is the same with morality. For both boys and girls the teacher must specify ideas and laws precisely. But if as a result morality is not defined in terms of a personal relationship, girls especially, because of their psychology, will not be stimulated by this legal morality.

It is very important to stress the relative way in which young girls are open to the general aspect of things. Though quite open to particular beings with whom they spontaneously and intuitively identify, girls only accede to universal realities and general laws through the mediation of a particular, personal and living reality. Thus, for girls, before being the universal Church and the six continents, the mystical body of Christ is the person of Jesus, the parish priest, the neighbors, the woman one helps out when she is sick. This becomes evident when we speak to girls about the structure of the Church, of the hierarchy, or of God's general attributes. While boys go from the universal to the particular, girls generally take the opposite route.

MASCULINE PSYCHOLOGY

The results of a study of the responses of boys are not as clear and decisive as those of girls in characterizing the dynamic axis around which their religious universe, their sense of God is organized. Their exploding juvenile imagination, their adolescent hyperemotive power, and their idealism ally them partly and for a while at least with certain traits of feminine psychology. Thus, especially at the time of adolescence and the beginning of late adolescence, person-to-person relationships are as important in the boy's religion as they are in the girl's religion. The teacher should be aware of this peculiarity which makes it possible for adolescent boys rather easily to follow catechetical programs oriented to girls, while the opposite is not true.[25]

Nevertheless, occasionally the study revealed, in addition to the characteristics common to boys and girls, the characteristics of the boy's religious universe. For him it is less a question of openness to a harmonious relationship with the person of God than of openness to nature and the order of things. In religion the boy seeks not so much a satisfying relationship with God as a support and dynamism for being and acting. At the same time he seeks a logical and coherent presentation of religion which will permit him to relate to God and to the world.

This is why many boys see God as the great motor and the great explanation of the world. Less turned toward the past and tradition than girls, they more spontaneously look to the future, to a realization of themselves in a projected scheme. Their religious synthesis is based on action. In the mentality of boys from vocational schools this solicitude for a synthesis based on action is accentuated. In contrast to boys from secondary schools, boys from vocational

[25] We have verified this several times, in particular in a program of catechesis on the Church. Both the boys and the girls were at ease in a discovery of the Church through the person of Jesus and of Christians. On the other hand, the following year, having tried to adopt another program based on the great realities of the Church in the world today, we found that the boys followed perfectly, while the girls manifested an unfeigned boredom.

schools seek not so much a universal explanation of religion as precise objectives and especially systematic laws for success and efficacy.

CONSEQUENCES

We have said that a presentation of Christianity in categories of person-to-person relationships satisfies the adolescent precisely because of his adolescence. But would it not be dangerous to insist too exclusively on this aspect? Do we not risk leaving the man of tomorrow ill equipped, ill at ease in a Christianity whose social and active aspects have not been sufficiently understood? And will this risk not become more serious as the technical mentality becomes more generalized?

In recent years, in reaction to a religious instruction devoid of personal involvement and encounter with life, schools and catechetical programs have been presenting revelation in "existential and interpersonal categories." Certain contemporary philosophical currents such as personalism and phenomenology have activated the reaction on the catechetical level and even on the theological level. Nevertheless it does not seem necessary to organize all presentation of religion around such axes. Such a presentation might not be adapted to certain temperaments and, in general, might not be sufficiently adapted to boys and men, especially to technicians.

Far from being discouraged, the catechist should realize that although some catechetical presentations have been necessary reactions to a certain period, they have not always been so well attuned to the technical period only lately opening up. Christianity will always involve person-to-person relationships, but these relationships, because they are lived by men in the world, presuppose a certain number of formulas, structures and precise laws. It is neither the structures nor the formulas which must be suppressed, but certain manners of expression and categories of thought. Thus for example, in place of the categories of classical philosophy, the modern catechist will be interested in substituting the categories of history, psychology, sociology, phenomenology and the sciences.

For boys there should be less stress on the relationship of *affective harmony* (which is suitable to girls) than on that of *participation in God's action through mission*. This, it seems to us, is a fundamental orientation for the catechesis of the modern boy.

INDICATIONS FOR CATECHESIS

If we push the preceding statements to their ultimate limit, we may well ask whether the responses to the questionnaire do not indicate a religion for boys and another for girls.

This situation would be unthinkable since monolithic or a priori interpretations may not be made. For a Christian, moreover, the incarnation reveals that divine reality is catholic, that it is offered and adapted to every human being. The God of Jesus Christ is given to both men and women, but he is not limited, not restricted to one or to the other.

In what sense, therefore, can the different ways of grasp-

ing religion among men and women demand a specially
adapted presentation?

First, the teacher, being aware of his students' "manner
of receiving," will carefully avoid the deviations to which
certain formulations, pictures and presentations can lead.
He should consider the way such words as "ideal" or
"father" are received. In catechesis he should utilize the
reflective thinking that characterizes youth between the
ages of 15 and 25. He should frequently correct or improve
his statements by encouraging his students to reflect on the
errors in their spontaneous mode of apprehension. This is
one of the most effective methods of teaching the faith to
adolescents.

Second, if the revealed message cannot change, he
should nevertheless adapt the perspective from which it is
presented to the milieu. The evangelists and the apostles
were the first to give us an example of this. The Pauline
synthesis is not set up around the same axes and with the
same stresses as the Johannine synthesis. It is the same with
the Augustinian and Thomistic syntheses. These masters
of the faith give an example of the way in which adapta-
tions can be made. It is not a question of choosing between
such and such a truth of revelation, but of presenting faith
in its essential, with *stresses and viewpoints* adapted to the
listener and the end envisioned.

It is not enough to stress boys' and girls' different points
of view. At the same time their complementary natures
must be stressed. "In the Lord woman needs man and man
needs woman,"[26] writes St. Paul. Here it could be asked
whether deviations in the masculine and feminine sense of

[26] See 1 Cor 11:11ff.

God would not have been corrected if these young people
had been educated in a life situation where the import of
the adult feminine and masculine world was balanced. Do
not tomorrow's technicians need to be influenced by the
religious values of the feminine world? Do not girls who
live in Christian boarding schools run by women have an
urgent need for the influence of militant adult Christians?
Would this not assure and objectify their faith and open
them to the Church's apostolic action in the world?

Psychologists note that the affective maturation of the
adolescent occurs partly as a result of his assimilation of
the characteristics proper to each sex. Such a truth should
influence religious education. The conversion of youth to
the God of Jesus Christ will occur insofar as the young
person has integrated not only the characteristics of his
own temperament, but also those of his sex, with his life
in Christ.

3. The Ethical Sense

*Why Speak of Morality and Ethics in Reference to the
Sense of God?* We might now ask whether the ethical
problem[27] is not foreign to the purpose of this discussion. At
first we thought we would not have to include it. But the
significance of the references and moral deductions expressed by adolescents in their relationship with God
forced this consideration.

[27] "Ethical sense" is a translation of the French word "*ethicité*,"
which has no English equivalent—tr.

After we discuss the link between the sense of God and morality for adolescents, we shall attempt to define the ethical sense.

In what does the adolescent's moral reference consist? In order to answer such a question it seems particularly helpful to consider not so much the differences according to age and sex, but the differences according to milieu.

1. *The Expressions.* The expressions used point to two things: 1. a strong predominance of the moral imperative among students from parochial schools and also among some students from technical schools; 2. the difference, in both motivation and quality of moral demands, between students from parochial and those from public schools.

First, let us consider the parochial schools, by way of examining some of the responses devolved from that milieu.[28]

"God is a master I must obey." "For me God is someone we must love and adore. We must serve him and he will reward us in heaven."

From these expressions three points may be stressed: 1. their proximity to the catechism formula: "we are made to know, love and serve God"; 2. the importance given the *imperative,* so that God is defined as "someone we *must* . . ."; 3. the interest in *reward,* whereby heaven is the prize for moral effort and is given in payment at the end of the labor.

[28] These statements were not chosen haphazardly. Intentionally they represent forceful expressions. Despite the sociological difference of the adolescents who responded to the investigation, an effort was made to choose statements which would characterize the entire group.

The following simple and classical diagram stresses the unfolding of man's dynamism. It also expresses, as in the statements above, God's sovereign rule. If the moral impulse seems to be the result of human reasoning, this reasoning begins with a consciousness of God's absolute rule.

God

↑

Me

This is not a question of a moral conduct whose dependence on the Holy Spirit is explicitly recognized, but rather of a virtuous impulse essentially demanded by the evidence of a God who is all. It is because God is the beginning and the end that a certain number of precepts should be followed, these being conceived as the way of returning to him. It is something like a ball that bounces back to the thrower after striking the opposite wall.

What is the case in the *public* schools? Here are two significant statements:

"God is a good father in whom we can confide everything."

"Our guide and comforter, the only one for whom life is worth living."

Three points can be noted here, the reverse of those of the parochial schools:

1. the *freedom of the formula*, its lack of reference to the catechism. It is a question of a reason to live, and the words used come from modern terminology;

2. also, the moral imperative takes on a *very secondary importance* or a much less categorical one. In the parochial schools, characteristic expressions were: "It is necessary"

or "I ought." In the public schools the students write: "We can" or "it is worth while," and an interpretation of all the responses to the questionnaire indicates that they would say: "it is good" or "it is normal";

3. finally, moral behavior seems to be more *affectively motivated* in public school students. Moral conduct does not seem to be the result of a reasonable consideration of God the creator, all powerful, and final end of creation. On the contrary, moral conduct is explicitly founded on the need for a subjective or even sympathetic accord between man and God, coupled with a need for success and happiness. The heart expresses a desire to live which is realized in a relationship with God whose essential characteristic is goodness and not omnipotence.

Another diagram is suggested:

$$God \xleftarrow{\hspace{1em}}\xrightarrow{\hspace{1em}} Me$$

Undoubtedly these two cases are never found in a pure state. But they have the advantage of forcefully characterizing the situation as a whole, or at least the latent tendencies among adolescents from different schools.

What can we conclude from these expressions of the sense of God?

1. During adolescence the moral aspect takes on such importance that it almost overshadows the other aspects of man's relationship with God. In both the public and private schools great importance was attached not necessarily to the moral imperative, which is above all a trait of the private schools, but to the moral reality.

2. The moral factor takes on extremely diverse character-

istics differentiated by age, sex and especially by the quality of education received in different schools. It can go from a healthy conception of morality to a very affective or, on the other hand, very rational and voluntarist moralism.

The deviation which affects the morality of many adolescents will later be spoken of at length. But it would seem unjust to characterize the adolescent's moral deficiency with the term "moralism." Thus we propose the term "ethical sense," which will be subject to less pejorative connotations.

The term "ethical sense" indicates the repercussion of moral behavior on the sense of God, and this in two ways:

1. the relationship with God is profoundly influenced, if not overshadowed, by subjective needs for moral excellence;

2. the moral impulse itself is principally controlled by the order of God the creator, rather than by the personal historical call of Jesus Christ.

2. *Adolescent Ethical Sense and Moralism.* A clarification of the meaning of morality will aid in a better understanding of the relationship between moral realities and the sense of God. What place should morality have in a Christian's relationship with God?

Let us first of all speak of the moral law. For a Christian the moral law is not the formulation of a more or less extrinsic absolute, a social necessity, or a condition and gauge of heavenly reward. On the level of conduct the moral law expresses precisely the demands of the existential relationship to which Christ gratuitously calls us.

Let us note that in any moral position, in any effort of human conduct, God has called man and man has responded through faith. This has placed man in a privileged existential and relational status with God. Before a Christian acts virtuously he receives God's envoy, Jesus Christ. In Christ man has been pardoned without meriting it, in Christ he has become the son of the Father and the brother of all men. All specifically Christian morality results from this grace-filled reality. As for natural morality, it is only the substratum of this law of grace, a substratum which results from man's creaturely condition which Christ has not destroyed but assumed.

From this perspective, the links between moral effort and the properly religious domain can be seen. For the Christian, moral effort does not originate in man's autonomous effort to reach the God of reason. It is first of all a recognition of the God of Jesus Christ and a response to the personal call of this God.

How does all this relate to the adolescent? Generally the relation of morality to the religious domain can be characterized in two ways:

1. As we have previously noted, adolescents are characteristically willing to remain on the level of natural morality, dependent on the God of the reason and the heart. Thus their moral effort does not appear as a response to a call of grace, as the acceptance of Jesus Christ, but as a subjective demand of the reason or of the heart trying to reach God.

2. Another characteristic frequently dominates the adolescent ethical sense. The adolescent is a being particularly drawn toward an ideal to be attained, toward his own success and the success of his relationships. This tension, un-

derlying his virtuous impulse and his moral effort, tends
to cloud his field of consciousness so that the impulse of
his will becomes much more important than the signs of
God's will.

In this regard Newman, remembering the year 1815
when he was 14 years old, wrote: "I thought that I was
more desirous of virtue than of piety. There was something
about piety that did not please me. And the idea of loving
God made no sense to me."[29] On the level of the faculties
involved in moral dynamism, the effort of the will tends to
supersede the effort to understand the intentions of the
Other. One could affirm: action tends to supersede con-
templation.

These two major characteristics of adolescent morality
tend to strain the quality of relationship with God. Adolescent morality is often too little dependent on the Spirit
of Christ. Subjective moral effort risks taking on more
importance than response to God's call. Certainly not all
adolescents fall into this danger. But it is typical of their
psychological desire for success. Precisely for this last
reason have we spoken of the ethical sense.

The ethical sense is often bent toward moralism. From
a Christian perspective moralism can be defined as a deviation which tends to disparage the reception of God in faith
and love, favoring a virtuous conduct principally governed
by natural, subjective or sociological needs. In the adolescent this deviation leads to an acceptance of moral obliga-
tion without a real understanding of its reference to super-

[29] Anne Morley, Lettres et Correspondance, 22.

natural reality or a recognition, through understanding and love, of its worth.

3. *Forms and Causes of the Adolescent Ethical Sense in the Public and Parochial Schools.* The principal cause of the adolescent ethical sense is psychological. At this age there is a drive toward self-realization, which can even go so far as a cult of prowess, and a need to identify with the group and environmental values. This has already been spoken of, so we shall not belabor the point. But turning to the distinction between the public and parochial schools, an analysis will be made of the particular forms and causes of the ethical sense.

a. *The ethical sense and its nuances among young people result from the type of educational authority they have experienced.*

The responses to the inquiry clearly pointed out the effects of the type of educational authority experienced. On the one hand, particularly in the public schools, a moral attitude was expressed in a euphoric, if not lax manner. On the other hand, particularly in the parochial schools, a sense of God and a moral attitude were frequently expressed in a voluntarist, or even in a rigoristic and Jansenistic manner. The following statements could characterize these attitudes: "It is worthwhile to love God," and "it is necessary." These statements represent the two different perspectives.

The following constants emerged from this study. When authority was stronger or constraining for the impulse of human subjectivity, the moral imperative became a more weighing demand. On the other hand, when authority was more discreet or silent in regard to the impulses of human subjectivity, the moral imperative was more supple, if not nonexistent. In the first instance a tyrannical superego dominated, whereas in the second a very attenuated superego resulted in a morality governed by subjective and social needs. In general the parochial school students were in the first category and the public school students in the second. Why?

Although the investigation revealed a great variety of individual tendencies, authority seemed to carry more weight in the parochial schools. Doubtless this is a result of the religious instruction given as well as the general educational framework. We must obey, we must go to catechism, we must go to Mass, etc. But other motives undoubtedly enter in and these are familial motives. In one case, for instance, a parent may feel very strongly about having his child educated at a parochial school, while another, more liberal parent may send his child to a public school.[30]

All these factors will lead to a more voluntarist ethical sense in the parochial schools, one more dependent on considerations of God's law. But in the public schools there will be an ethical sense more dependent on the demands for subjective success.

b. *Especially in its aspect of individual and voluntary moralism does the ethical sense issue in great part from educational emphases.*

First of all, let us stress the great importance of the mundane moral atmosphere which surrounds modern adolescents—for example, slogans such as "succeed," "keep

[30] Many parents of adolescents in public schools may be demanding in educational matters, but it seems that this demand takes a different form.

young," etc.[31] In an investigation conducted by the Parisian newspaper *L'Express* on the "new wave," it was noted that the moral objective of the average Frenchman consisted in satisfying his ideal self-image. For the adolescent it consisted in realizing his profound subjective tendencies; for the adult, in being recognized by society. We should never forget that the adolescent lives in a specific moral milieu, that he breathes in his moral environment and assimilates its demands.

But it does not suffice to criticize the times. The religious teaching received should also be considered. Many children have been formed by the catechism: but the catechism has not been based on God's call. Rather it has been based on the objective needs of individual salvation. These needs are at once psychological and in line with the adolescent's thought, but they differ from the dynamic perspective of salvation history. Let us briefly recall the structure of the catechism:

1. *what we must believe.* Understood: accomplishment of the fundamental problem of salvation. How many will thus be tempted to conceive dogma itself as an ensemble of beliefs destined to keep us on the road to heaven!

2. *what we must do.* Laws and commandments are conceived as methods, rather than as signs from a God who calls us to the fullness of life;

3. *the means to be used.* Among these grace and the sacraments are no longer seen as the initiatives and accomplishments of God in us. Rather than as gifts of

---

[31] It suffices to read the ads in any weekly journal.

God, they are seen prosaically as things to be used, methods
for attaining a given end.

This perspective, centered on the effort to resolve the
problem of salvation, leads adolescents more or less consciously to emphasize the importance of their moral behavior. It is not surprising that at its extreme, this perspective sees man as more important than God. Certainly the
catechism does not contain any erroneous statements. But
its internal structure, based on the problem of individual
salvation, is such that in the psychology of the young
people who study it man ends up occupying first place.

It might be countered that many children today have not
had this classical form of catechetical instruction. This is
true, and it is evident in the responses that emanate from
certain schools. But in these relatively rare cases another
question arises: what place has been given to morality in
those catechisms more solidly based on the sources of revelation? Perhaps the tendency has been to go from one extreme to another, and no longer to consider morality. This
study, however, did not attempt to judge the effects of
modern catechetics.

4. *Pedagogical Perspectives.* The adolescent ethical sense
presents at once a value and a serious hazard.

It is a value, for more than at other ages the adolescent
cannot stand passively before the concept of God. The
adolescent must choose for or against God in his own life.
He can not acquiesce to an abstract notion but must
progress: "An eternal nomad progressing toward God,"
said Saint-Exupéry.

From then on adolescents will imbue their conception of God with affective impulses or a loving involvement of their life, and this is a positive factor. Even if these impulses toward God are very little purified at first, they should be regarded sympathetically. Is the God of Jesus Christ not a God of the covenant? There are teachers who uniformly criticize the Boy Scouts, for example, saying that such idealism and activity lead more to natural heroism than to Christian holiness. Naturally any unconscious slipping into a natural morality or natural concept of God must be denounced. But the direct target of these denunciations should not be adolescents. The first purpose of such considerations is to provoke healthy self-criticism among teachers.

Teachers should depend, in the manner of God as revealed by Jesus Christ, on adolescent voluntarism in order to develop an authentically Christian religious fervor. The teacher should understand these more or less conscious and passing deviations, which are certainly preferable to a lukewarm or passive freedom.

Alerted by a critical analysis of the situation, the teacher should at the same time be clear on the ambiguities and dangers of this ethical sense. With its tension toward God and its serious observance of a certain law in order to attain this end, its voluntarism and spontaneous asceticism, adolescence is analogous to the time when the Jews awaited the Messiah. The great danger of this stage is Pharisaism. In many ways the adolescent can be compared to the Pharisee—not to the hypocritical Pharisee denounced in the gospel, but to the Pharisee pointed out by St. Paul. In fact, like this latter Pharisee, the adolescent burns a little with the cult of the law. He possesses a zeal striving for self-fulfillment, a fervor for the cause, intransigeance, violence, an intensified idea of his own worth, and a jealous cult of his own prerogatives. Is this entirely evil? No, but the adolescent runs the risk of taking himself too seriously and being so much a prisoner of his own wisdom and efforts that he cannot accept the Messiah as he is.

The Christian community must teach the adolescent the primary importance of listening to God's word. The word of God must be proclaimed to the adolescent in such a way that his moral effort will not be seen as a subjective striving for his own ideal, but as a response to a God who calls him. This can be summed up with the slogan: the indicative before the imperative. Catechesis should always firmly proclaim God's marvels in the midst of men before imposing a code of conduct.

GENERAL CONCLUSION

These considerations of naturation, egomorphism and the ethical sense have continually stressed the danger of religious immanentism. God is not a man, nor is he an idealized adolescent. Perhaps this analysis will lead to an understanding of the ways in which man, at different ages in his life, places God at the service of his ego.

The pedagogical orientation which most clearly emerges from this study is that, rather than in man's own invention, God must be sought where he speaks. In this way the primacy of revelation will be given, as much as possible, its proper value in the eyes of young people.

3. God as a Father

The concept of fatherhood undoubtedly represents the most important and most sensitive point in this study* of the sense of God among adolescents.

This is an important concept, for statistically speaking from 45 to 50 per cent of those responding used the term "father" to define God. Again, it is especially important because the word "father" is at the heart of Christian revelation. Finally, it is important because a certain number of key words crystalize around the word "father," words which require clarification: "creator," master," "love."

But fatherhood is a sensitive point since one might wonder if young Christians understand the word "father" in its true Christian context.

For these reasons it seems advantageous to study this aspect in itself. At the same time, it seems to us that this study should represent a sort of synthesis of our thought; not because it sums up our analyses in any great detail, but because it goes to the heart of an essential problem: the sense of God's immanence and transcendence for adolescents.

First, the data and their motivational causes should be

* The author wishes to thank Abbé G. Duperray and Mlle. G. Dechancé for their collaboration in the preparation of this chapter.

examined. When young Christians speak of their Father in heaven, what exactly do they mean? In what way does the meaning of "Father" evolve with age? What is the meaning and import of terms generally associated with the concept of father, that is, the words "creator," "master" and "love"? Why do adolescents apprehend God in this way?

A comparison of the biblical concept of creation and fatherhood with that expressed by adolescents will follow. Finally, an analysis of how these concepts affect the adolescent's idea of God and Christian life will be made, and some pedagogical implications noted.

1. Data and Causes

Two Important Parallel Courses. The concept of fatherhood among young people proffers, in a general way, two important meanings which do not seem to be linked:

—father could mean *creator;*

—father could mean *love* in the sense of all-powerful, forceful and beneficial goodness.

1. GOD AS A CREATOR

The Data. About half the responses in the study indicated that the word "Father" was associated with "Creator" or even with "Master."[1] This constant association of words

---

[1] The percentage of responses which represent paternity in terms of creation and power persists, in almost equal proportion, from preadolescence to late adolescence. We arrived at this evaluation after numerous studies of the different groups of responses, especially those of adolescents and late adolescents.

led to the inference of a certain identity, if not confusion of concepts. In the majority of cases the word "Father" meant first of all "He who made me," and then "the transcendent Master who rules." ("Father of the world"—pre-adolescence; "Father of all men," "a Father, the Master of all things"—late adolescence.)

Generally the word "Creator" appeared first, followed by that of "Father," and often by that of "Master."

"God is the Creator of all things. He is a demanding Father for those who wish to follow him" (16-year-old boy, public school).

"God is the Creator and sovereign Master" (12-year-old boy, public school).

"God is the creator of the world, our sovereign Master" (16-year-old boy, public school).

Sometimes the two terms "Creator" and "Father" seem to include one another in the mind of the adolescent, so that they were linked, almost spontaneously, by a coordinating conjunction in one phrase:

"God is our Creator and thus our Father" (17-year-old girl, public school).

"He is our Creator and therefore our Father" (16-year-old boy, vocational school).

Father, Master, Creator. These three terms do not always appear as such. However, the concept and fundamental relationship remain. Only the formulation changes. The following phrases illustrate this point:

"God is the Creator, he to whom we owe our lives, the Master of all things" (17-year-old boy, public school).

"God—the all powerful creator who desired to give us life" (15-year-old boy, public school).

In this context it can be seen that fatherhood does not first of all mean love, but power. In reality, "Creator," "Father" and "Master" appear as closely related terms, if not almost as synonyms. They point above all to the priority of God in relation to man and to the dependence of all existence on him. Let us attempt to answer in depth this question: *why are the words "God," "Creator," "Father" and "Master" so closely related?*

The Psychological Factor. The more or less conscious and spontaneous reasoning of young people could be summarized as follows: God is Father *because* he is the *author* of creation, and God is Master *because* he has the rights of an *author*.[2] This seems to be the most fundamental common point, as well as the most general, regarding the concept of God among adolescents. The reasoning is simple and natural. It touches without any reflective detour or rationalization the classic proofs of God's existence. Actually the reasoning is rooted in the most universal and perhaps most profound human experience, the experience of one's original dependence on a father and mother.

One might well wonder at this point why the expression "God is the *author* of *creation*" was used rather than "creator." The reason is that the responses neither expressed nor showed understanding of the theological and Christian concept of creation. God was not seen as he who eternally causes the existence of beings and things. He was seen as someone who one day made man and the world.

[2] We do not claim that such reasoning is purely spontaneous. It is certain that it is supported, if it was not acquired, by teaching. It is no less true that this reasoning is psychologically fundamental. This is what is stressed here.

Is the biblical image of a God making man from the earth, much as the artist makes a statue, as dominant in adolescents' minds as it is badly understood? Apparently so. In their conception of creation adolescents undoubtedly surpass the common concept of the fabrication of a thing, but they do not surpass the concept of their own birth from their parents. In other words, adolescents base their explanation of creation on their experience and understanding of their own birth—in the full sense of the word, meaning procreation and education. This is the first and fundamental reason why fatherhood and creation are so frequently binominous.

For the same reason the concept of creation and fatherhood are linked with that of *absolute rule*. God is master because he has created all, that is, we depend on him as a child depends on the one from whom he received his being and his life.

One last point should be made. Adolescence is an age of breaking away from the father, if not an age of revolt against him and the authority he represents. It is very possible, therefore, that an accentuated sensitivity at this age to the terrestrial father's power contaminates or at least conditions one's concept of the heavenly Father. Insofar as his relationship with a demanding parental authority is his present problem, the adolescent conceives God the Father as an *author of life having full powers*.

"God is a superior person to whom we owe our life, the Master of all things."

"God is our Father. For me, it is he who controls everything."

"God is all that rules us."

Do not such expressions, which are very common especially among boys, manifest a certain relational crisis with the earthly father?

The Teaching Factor. Although it is experimentally unverifiable on a large scale, it is impossible not to note a second important motive for the "Creator-Father-Master" association, namely the motivation of the instruction received. Confrontation with young Protestants as well as reminiscence of the formulas taught (in Catholic schools) leads to this conclusion. Why?[3]

The Formulas. "I believe in God the Father almighty . . ." (a linking of Father-Power). So begins the Creed. And what does the catechism say? The traditional text used in French dioceses reads: "God is a pure spirit, infinitely good, infinitely perfect, Creator and Sovereign Master of all things" (Here the word "Father" is not mentioned, but only the association, "Creator-Master"). Likewise, the Baltimore Catechism reads: "God is the supreme being. . . . When we say that God is almighty we mean that he can do all things."

Such formulas, of course, influence the notion of God among children and adolescents. In their responses to the

---

[3] A study of the notion of God was made among one hundred and six Protestant adolescents. They represented two groups, one corresponding to parochial schools because of their religious education, the other corresponding to public schools and more spontaneous in their expression. Above all, an insistence on God as Jesus Christ the Savior was noted, with an accent on a tragic sense of man unable to save himself. Second, they were much more influenced by the Bible in their expression, indicating both their education and their *aptitude for biblical concepts.* In addition, there were a variety of subjective and natural influences.

investigation, many of the youths, even among the oldest, turned to something like the memorized formulas.

"God who is my Master, is a pure spirit, infinitely perfect, good and adorable" (16-year-old boy).

"God is an eternal Spirit, infinitely perfect and good, the Creator and Master of all things" (14-year-old boy).

The "Natural" Orientation of Teaching. But much more is involved here. For Protestants also have the Creed. They do not, however, express themselves in the same way as Catholics. Besides, in the Creed the notion of fatherhood is primary. It comprises creation and culminates in Jesus Christ. On the other hand, the catechism gives a definition for God which does not even contain the word "Father." Therefore how can we say that the association "Creator-Father" comes uniquely from teaching?

It is not so much the formula as such which has so much influence, but the framework and general orientation which Catholic education has had for so long. Whether it is a question of sermons or the internal structure of the catechism, teaching has been based less on a biblical view of God's personal call to man than on the view of man's own striving toward God, the course of him who tries to resolve the problem of his salvation.[4] Here one can think of the National French Catechism or the Baltimore Catechism. The beginning point, the psychological lever which attempts to govern the dynamism of

[4] J. A. Jungman, *Handing on the Faith*, New York 1962. "Everything that is presented in this catechism is correct, but it only glances at man's needs, his searching and his endeavors; it is a subjective and narrow aspect of divine reality" (139).

the religious understanding of young students, is not so much a response to Jesus' call to the kingdom as it is a response to a subjective need for salvation.

What is the result? First of all, as we have already noted, when we stress man's progress in this way, man rather than God assumes primary importance.[5] Furthermore, and this is the more important, even if God maintains primary importance, who is this God? At the end of a course based above all on man, one risks discovering only the God of man.

That the God of Judeo-Christian revelation is not opposed to the God of reason is certain. But in order to discover him it is necessary to go beyond the procedures of subjective seeking. Too many young people seem to adhere to the latter way of knowing God. One could say that they are incapable of liberating themselves from a teaching which has perhaps insisted too much on rational methods for attaining God.

Did not St. Paul, in his First Epistle to the Corinthians (1:17–26), show that the wordly thinker, the one wise according to the flesh, has not recognized "the mysterious and hidden wisdom of God"? Did he not thus preach "Christ crucified," and "the folly of the gospel"?

It would seem that Christian teaching has nearly forgotten these gospel and Pauline perspectives. Instead of using reason to better understand revelation, have not teachers sometimes unconsciously tried to gain revelation through reason?

[5] This does not mean that works are useless for discovering God. What is criticized here is too great a stress on man.

Perhaps in their catechesis on God teachers have been too content with the procedures of philosophical thought so-called and as a consequence have not sufficiently considered biblical thought. Karl Rahner distinguishes the two procedures thus:

A cosmological metaphysics ascends to a first cause of the world, to an intellectual first cause, and thence to a first cause transcending the world, and thus (in principle, at least) proceeds until it has in fact achieved some understanding of God as Person (in purely formal terms, of course); in this way it terminates in the ultimate question as to whether and how this personal God might not only continue to cause the world but also—appearing alongside the world, as it were—might wish to deal with it. The development of the Old Testament conception of God proceeds in exactly the reverse order: first comes the experience of God as a free Person active in the world, a Person generous and abundant, who reveals himself in his proper name, who calls and chooses; and it is only from this historical experience of who Yahweh is that it becomes progressively clearer what he is—not just a God, not just a powerful Lord in the history of perhaps this people alone, but the Lord of the history of all peoples and so the Lord of Nature too: the transcendent, spiritual Cause and Source of all reality, lifted up above every earthly limitation.[6]

Of course one would not wish, as a reaction, to deny the value of philosophical labor, or to oust it from catechesis. A balanced understanding of faith presupposes natural knowledge and an unfolding of philosophical reflection. But catechesis on God should not be overly limited to philosophical procedures.

With the catechetical renewal these perspectives have most assuredly been reconsidered. But have the principle

[6] *Theological Investigations* 1, 93.

of synthesis, the point of view and the fundamental orientation truly undergone the requisite transformation?[7] In sum, besides the catechetical formulas which could have been borrowed from theodicy—for example, the catechism's concept of God—it is above all the general orientation of the teaching which, with its psychological factors, seems to motivate the adolescent's tendency practically to reduce the concept of Father to that of author of creation. These psychological factors lead to a God in the image of man. And religious teaching which is too natural leads to the God of philosophers and scholars.

2. A God of Love

The Data. God is Father and Love. Such expressions were found in about 10 per cent of the responses. Among a certain number, the girls in particular, no concept of creation was expressed at all. God's fatherhood seemed to be linked to his almighty and beneficent goodness toward man.

"God is our omnipotent Father who loves me very much" (14-year-old girl).

"For me God is a loving Father who understands me, a Father very near who comforts me when I feel alone, deserted" (13-year-old girl).

The concept of a God of Love seems spontaneously to exclude the concept of God a Creator. Why? It is difficult to ascertain reasons, but in studying all the responses of

[7] The German *A Catholic Catechism* (New York 1962) certainly reverses this orientation. But in France or the U.S.? And how much more time will it take for the effects of this change in orientation to be felt on the level of the masses?

an individual it often seems that an adolescent is exclusively centered on affective relationships.

Nevertheless it should be noted that this love does not systematically exclude other realities such as justice or severity. One could even affirm that, in general, when adolescents note "God's great goodness," they almost instinctively amend it with his justice:

"God is a very good Father, severe, but just, and he loves every one of his creatures" (15-year-old girl).

"God is a very good Father, but just and severe" (15-year-old boy).

What Causes This Link between Fatherhood and Love? Why do a certain number of adolescents tend to define fatherhood almost exclusively in terms expressing love, benevolence and even proximity?

In replying to the questionnaire, girls especially linked love and fatherhood. Furthermore, statistically speaking, as girls mature they tend to define God more in terms of love, and this in exactly inverse proportion to boys. Following are the percentages of boys and girls at different ages who define God in terms of love.

	Boys	Girls
Preadolescence	67.	51.65
Pubescent Adolescence	45.	62.35
Late Adolescence	41.	75.

How can one account for the stronger link between fatherhood and love among girls? In large part this link is due to the influence of psychological differences between boys and girls. The girl subconsciously transfers her need for paternal security and "an ideal man" to God. She functions in the categories of affective relationships. The

boy is characterized by his developing need to rule the
earth and to assert himself in face of authority. As a consequence his idea of divine fatherhood is expressed less in
affective terminology, and if he should describe fatherhood
in terms of love this is probably the result of his individual
temperament or particular experience. Thus we conclude
once again with the importance of psychological factors
in the expression of the adolescent's notion of God.

RECAPITULATING TABLE

A series of graphs will make possible a rather precise comparison of the different terms associated with the word
"God" at different ages.

2. Revelation and the Concept of God
as Father-Creator

A PEDAGOGICAL REFLECTION

The Importance of the Crisis of Filial Sentiments in the
Development of the Religious Sense. Pierre Bovet once
wrote: "Religious sentiment is filial sentiment. For the
child the first object of this sentiment is his parents. The
father and mother are the child's gods. They have all the
divine perfections. But life's experience forces the child to
alter, if not his religion, at least his god. He must transfer
the marvelous attributes he first gave to his parents to a
more remote being."[8]

[8] P. Bovet, Le sentiment religieux et la psychologie de l'enfant,
Paris 1925, 29. See also H. Carrier, The Sociology of Religious Belonging, New York 1965, 117–137.

Preadolescence	Pubescent Adolescence	Late Adolescence
First Pole: the Father, God of Creation (Father-Creator-Master)		
More academic	More affective	More affective and intellectual
12 to 13 years	14 to 16 years	17 to 20 years
A rather "in-self" notion not linked with man:	Relationships of dependence, *affectively* and rather *individually* sensed:	Relationships of dependence *vitally* sensed on the individual level, but also on the social and cosmic levels:
"The Father of all men."	"My father."	"Our Father, absolute Master."
Providence	Father-Providence who is concerned about us.	Father-Providence on a *universal* scale
Guide	Father-Guide who shows us the way and who accompanies us.	
Judge	Father-Judge who sees, surveys and sanctions	A less individual perspective
Supreme Being: God is pure Spirit (rather academic)		Supreme Being (more philosophical, responding to a need of the person)
A Mystery: academic (no questions are posed)	So much so that it is impossible to *sense* him	*Mysterious* Father for man (doubts; intellectual unknown outside of man's grasp)
Second Pole: the Father, God of the Ego		
More academic	More affective	More affective and intellectual concept
12 to 13 years	14 to 16 years	17 to 20 years
The Father, God of the Heart (very little noted)	*The Father,* strength and support, confidant, consoler, friend, comrade	*Confidant,* object of impulses of the heart and the seeking of the Spirit
Third Pole: the Father Whose Paternity Is Revealed to Us in Jesus Christ		
Formulas learned (rare)	"God is good, but he is just. He has sent his son to save us" (very rare)	Revealed fatherhood is assimilated in a vital way (very rarely expressed)

It is difficult to reduce religious sentiment to a simple sublimation of filial sentiment. On this point Bovet's thought is assuredly contestable. It would seem it is impossible to reduce Christianity to some natural development of filial sentiment. However there is an *essential* relationship between filial sentiment and the sense of God. This exists not in an inductive manner—for example, God the sublimation of the earthly father—but in a deductive manner. The earthly father is a sign of the heavenly Father.

One must certainly agree with Bovet's contention that such a study is at the heart of any psychology of the religious sense. Did we not just point out the links between the concept of fatherhood and those of creation, omnipotence and love? If the crises in a child's relations with his parents always mark crucial stages in the purification of his concept of God, how much more is this true of the adolescent's crisis. Bovet analyzes the consequences of the first crisis of "life experience" occuring around the age of 6, for the sense of God. How much more reason is there for speaking of the crisis between the ages of 14 and 20. The latter crisis seems much more grave because it is more conscious and constitutes a much more profound break from the parents.

A Comparison. The findings of this study have shown how much the adolescent's sense of God's fatherhood is dependent on subjective experience, teaching and especially filial experience. This notion comprises at once an *idea of creation*, of the dependence of his being on his very birth, and a *concept of love* based on his experience of filial love for his parents.

Now, faced with this adolescent conception of God,

what does Christian revelation say of God's fatherhood, of
his almighty rule, of creation? A comparison of the heavenly and earthly fatherhoods may help clarify this point.

Our heavenly Father is "signified" by our earthly father.
Such is the fundamental analogy underlying this study.[9]
Like every analogy, this one also has two aspects. *An aspect
of similitude:* God the Father is in some way similar to
our earthly father; *an aspect of discontinuity,* of radical
difference: God is not at all like our earthly father.

A study of these two aspects will be followed by a reflection on the position of adolescents, and on the deviations, dangers and limits they incur, when faced with
Christian revelation.

1. *God the Father Is in Some Way Similar to Our
Earthly Father.* To begin with, and in accord with adolescent thought, the Bible presents *creation* as the *foundation
of God's fatherhood.* Isaiah associates the image of the
Father as Creator of the earth and heavens with the image
of the potter fashioning a vase of clay: "Yet, O Lord, you
are our father; we are the clay and you the potter: we are
all the work of your hands" (64:7). This view, characteristic of the Old Testament, is also found in the religions
of some pagans. Thus Plato says that God is "the Father
of the universe."

Besides this notion of creative paternity another is found
in the Old Testament, one which expands in the New and

---

[9] We must be agreed on widening the concept of Father to the
encompassing concept of "parents." Mircea Eliade, in *Images and
Symbols* (New York 1961) has shown, in line with psychoanalysis,
to what extent the father and mother must not be taken as individual limited realities, but as images of a wider content and
multiple forms.

especially characterizes a fatherhood of benevolence and loving solicitude: "When Israel was a child I loved him, out of Egypt I called my son" (Hos 11:1).

This father image is manifested in the spontaneous expressions of a considerable number of adolescents. No doubt certain pagans also had this conception. Does it not echo this phrase of St. Paul: ". . . I bend my knees to the Father of our Lord Jesus Christ, from whom all fatherhood in heaven and on earth receives its name" (Eph 3:14–15)?

In this way Christian revelation ratifies the notion of a Father-Creator, which is based on the human experience of filiation and paternity. And revelation demonstrates the principle of the analogy of philosophies. Is this surprising? Not really, for the revelation of Jesus Christ elevates the order of creation to a more wondrous state.

2. *God Is in Some Way Totally Unlike Our Earthly Father.*

a. *God's Fatherhood in Christian Revelation.* God is not exactly like our earthly father. He is not a creator and master in the same way as parents. These statements, in appearance so simple, are in fact so often contested and their transcendence so difficult to comprehend that they constitute one of the most original, insistent and violent currents of Christ's preaching. "Call no man Father . . . Do not be called Master . . . You have only one Master . . . Do not command in the manner of heads of nations who cause their rule to be felt."

Jesus knows of whom he speaks when he speaks of God, of the Authority, of the Father. It is *"his* Father." He came that men might have this understanding and that thus radically renewed by his Spirit they might be able to say like him, with him: *Abba, Father!* In order to grasp the radical newness of Jesus' message it certainly does not suffice to detail the meaning of words such as "Father" and "filial adoption." What is important is to live in Jesus Christ, in the radical consciousness of anOther known through grace.

In fact, the *via negationis* of the philosophers does not procure any new element for defining God. It only indicates that there is a break to be made somewhere, anOther to present. What Other? The philosopher will never say. It is Jesus, and historical revelation will introduce us to the mystery of this Other. How? Certainly not with new words, but by giving us the Holy Spirit of God himself. The break expressed by Jesus consisted essentially in telling us that it is not only in the broadening of a human experience, whatever it might be (even the most unthinkable), that we discover God the Father, but by listening to him, by becoming disciples of and sons in him. This reality is hidden from the wise and revealed to little ones. In other words, instead of simply placing us in the presence of creation, Jesus places us face to face *with himself*, better yet, *he places us in himself*. This is the essential break. And from this point on, from the point of this break, we are placed in grace as hearers of the word. Jesus now speaks, through analogy (the only way it can be said!), the infinite excellence of his Father.

Because of the grace of Christ's revelation the similitude is exceeded, and the way to the Absolute acquires a direction, a quality, a certitude and a content which transcends philosophy. This is verified by the words man uses to define

God and the comportment of his life in relation to God. In describing such realities human language is completely inadequate. However even the stammering expressions of adolescents are not devoid of meaning.

A glance at apostolic revelation, particularly the Epistle to the Galatians,[10] will perhaps lead to a deeper understanding of our life in God. An examination of the consequences of this revelation in our lives will aid in this understanding. In this way the newness and transcendent quality of the heavenly Father will best be understood. Three points are relevant:

1. *Possession of the Inheritance.* Our inheritance is not an indeterminate pagan heaven, but *life with God in Jesus Christ.* The inheritance is a life of friendship with the resurrected Jesus Christ, "participation in the divine nature even now before the fullness of glory." "No longer do I call you servants . . . but friends" (Jn 15:15). "For you are all the children of God through faith in Christ Jesus" (Gal 3:26).

The immediate effect of this participation is an introduction to a new type of relationship with God. No longer are we related to God by fear, remoteness and ignorance as are the pagans. Our relationship with God is ruled by *assurance, the certitude of being loved and heard,* the certitude of Jesus when he said to his Father: "I know well

[10] See Gal 4:4–8: "But when the fullness of time came, God sent his Son, born of a woman, born under the law, that he might redeem those who were under the law, that we might receive the adoption of sons. And because you are sons, God has sent the Spirit of his Son into our hearts, crying Abba, Father. So that he is no longer a slave, but a son; and if a son, an heir also through God."

that you always answer me." Considering the extraordinary
quality of freedom given through participation in the Spirit
of Jesus, the first Christians used a Greek word to characterize this Christian life: *parrhesis*: that is, the democratic
life, a life comprising the right to say all with an assurance
of being taken seriously. St. Paul says: "So we too . . . were
enslaved under the elements of the world," but now
"Christ has made us free" (Gal 4:3, 5:1).

2. A corollary to the freedom of the sons of God
is the *gratuitous pardon* given us by God in Jesus Christ,
and therefore by his revelation to us. The supreme perfection of the Father consists in his mercy. We are no longer
"the cursed," but "the pardoned" on whom a "great love"
reposes.

3. Finally, sonship in Jesus Christ gathers Christians as brothers into a holy people. Filial relationship with
God is not a matter for one individual; a whole people is
chosen. It is a chosen people, it is the Church who says
tenderly to her God: *Abba!* "There is neither Jew nor
Greek; there is neither slave nor freeman; there is neither
male nor female. For you are all one in Christ Jesus" (Gal
3:28).

How far it is from simple considerations of human sonship to the fullness of sonship we are called to by the one
whom John calls the Son of God!

b. *Creation in Christian Revelation.* Another point
also merits attention. It has been noted that adolescents
often link creation and paternity. This is true in the Old
Testament but less mentioned in the New Testament,
centered as it is on sonship in Jesus Christ.

How does Christian revelation understand the idea of

creation? Here again, how important it is to go beyond the
aspect of similarity expressed in analogies centered on
birth, development or fabrication.

When the Bible speaks of creation it undoubtedly
stresses the fact that the world only exists through God.
But this dependency does not alienate man. On the contrary, "what is realized from the beginning of the Old
Testament is the intransigeance of Israel's belief in the
living God as the only source of life. This is their central
teaching and it is never eclipsed."[11] This notion originates
from the fact of creation. "He did not create it to be a
waste but designed it to be lived in" (Is 45:18). God is
fertile, God is source, God is the producer of life. And it
is in this way that he is radically different from man. "Of
old you established the earth, and the heavens are the
work of your hands. They shall perish, but you remain
though all of them grow old like a garment. Like clothing
you change them, and they are changed, but you are the
same, and your years have no end" (Ps 101:26–29).

God appears in the Bible with strength and an impres-
sive authority, but the transcendence which is linked with
this power and authority is first of all a transcendence of
life. God is always bursting forth, man is a "weed which
begins to droop the evening of its birth." In this sense
God's transcendence does not annihilate human vitality,
but is its source. To receive God is to live, to be free, to
stand straight! Here one of the most fundamental of
biblical themes is touched upon. "I the Lord, am your God

[11] Paul-Marie de la Croix, l'Education du sens de Dieu, Paris
1960, 42.

who led you forth from the land of Egypt; open wide your mouth and I will fill it" (Ps 80:11).

The New Testament asserts the same thing. "In him was the *life*," writes St. John. "I have come that they may have life . . ." The prologue affirms in dynamic and precise terms: "He gave them the power to *become* sons of God."

Perhaps the reader feels that we have parted from the idea of creation to the idea of life and source of life. But the discussion reflects the emphasis given in the Bible, and an accent which reacts against the too facile interpretations of human analogies of creation. How many adolescents spontaneously think—and their crisis drives them to it— that being born of a father and a mother, far from freeing and vivifying them, renders them prisoners? For them living and being free consist in being emancipated from the guardianship of their parents, while, in the Bible, living and being free consist in being "God's exclusive property."

The Adolescent Situation

The Adolescent's Fixation: the Analogy of Human Fatherhood. What, one might ask, is the situation of adolescents in view of Christian revelation?

First of all, this investigation revealed that adolescents have a heightened sensitivity to similarities between different levels of being. This is a very positive note insofar as it opens a route toward a natural conception of God and, in a general way, toward the spiritual world. But even on this level, this "symbolic sensitivity" is not without danger.

Actually the adolescent tends to confuse God's transcendence with the absolute of an analogy. He does not say: God's paternity is of another category, another dimension than that of my father. Rather he says: God's paternity is my father's paternity pushed to the absolute. God is not the altogether Other. He is stronger, better, more tender. He possesses all my father's qualities to an infinite degree.

This is a sort of "absolute immanence" which puts true transcendence in the wrong light.[12]

This leads us to the second point which could have far-reaching consequences. Adolescents tend to be *overly attached* to the *aspect of similarities*. They do not seem very open to a paternity which would be of another order and another quality. It could be said that they are settled in this attitude, and the results of the study bear this out. Is this a consequence of their sensitivity to symbolism? Is this due to a religious teaching which is not sufficiently Christian? Or again, is it a consequence of an affective block in which the earthly father obscures the image of the heavenly Father? Let us not linger with the causes. Undoubtedly all three causes are involved.

What is important is an examination of the underlying images, the forms of sensitivity, and the follies which result from the adolescent's fixation. This attachment to the analogy of human paternity unconsciously leads to a false sense of God which has literally poisoned or arrested

[12] More precisely it could be said that adolescents, in this passage to the Absolute, do not make a break. And this is only one case of the fundamental psychological attitude of the adolescent who does not surpass his own ego nor the direction of his tendencies to open up to anOther.

the growth of many Christians, while at the same time
giving rise to very ardent criticism on the part of non-
Christians.

The Dangers of This Fixation. It is especially in the
blocking of "Creator-Father-Master" that the consequences
seem most dangerous. If the adolescent's idea of creation
and omnipotence is too limited to the personal experience
he has of paternity, his sense of God can be affected in
several ways.

1. *Tendency To Be Limited by a Natural Conception of
Divine Sonship.* For adolescents, the idea of supernatural
sonship is overshadowed by a totally natural conception of
creature-child. In the responses of 2000 adolescents, sonship in Christ was hardly mentioned at all!

2. *Tendency To Be Limited by a False Conception of
Creation.* Adolescents consider creation as a completed
act which took place once and for all in time, much like
their own birth. Thus their dependence on God the
creator does not appear to them as a dynamic dependence
which allows them to collaborate in this creative action
with an active consent by which they fully become themselves. Rather this dependence appears as a sort of passive
receptivity which should be broken away from as quickly
as possible, much as the dependent adolescent seeks adult
maturity in freedom from his father.

3. *Tendency To Imagine God on the Basis of Strong
Affective Reactions.* Insofar as his relationship with his
parents has been unhappy, the adolescent in his concept of
God-Father-Creator risks being tarnished if not falsely
idealized as a compensation. On the other hand, when the

experience of fatherhood has been happy, the adolescent's concept of God the Creator, the great ruler of the universe, will be amended with the concept of his tenderness. Perhaps this is the reason adolescents sometimes make such statements as:

"He created us, but he is also our Father." "He is a master, but he is good."

In these two cases, the affective reaction is such that it tends to "construct God" according to the processes of formal thought, which we shall study later.

4. *Tendency To Misunderstand God's Transcendence.* For many adolescents, especially the older ones, God's transcendence is essentially expressed in images of domination, remoteness and priority, all images linked with a concept of Father-Creator.

"God is our Father. For me, it is he who governs everything" (16-year-old student).

"If man is to obey, he must be afraid of something. This is God" (16-year-old student).

"God is the superior person to whom we owe our lives" (18-year-old student).

Such emphases recurred frequently in the responses and a sort of fatalism gradually became evident. Here especially any attachment to an overly natural and unique conception, or perhaps we should say to a devious conception, should be deplored. It is most difficult to lead adolescents to a correct understanding of transcendence. This difficulty is due to the complex analogies the human mind is forced to borrow in order to arrive at a conception of transcendence. Philosophically the term "transcendence" means that God is radically different from creation, "absolutely independent of the universe he created by a free act of his will."[13] Belot says that a reality can be said to transcend another when it possesses two characteristics: "1. That it is superior to it, belongs to a higher state in the hierarchy, and 2. that it cannot be attained through continuous progress."[14]

In itself, this philosophical notion is neither opposed to the idea of God as the Creator of life and freedom, nor to that of a God present to man through love. However it is ambiguous. The images it borrows—discontinuity, hierarchy and superiority—are so closely related to unhappy human experiences of authority that man spontaneously misunderstands the notion of transcendence. For example, Leibniz characterized God's transcendence in the following expressions: "In relation to man, God is what an inventor is to his machine, what a prince is to his subjects, and even what a father is to his children" (Monadology 84). There is a bit of humor in the final expression: "and even what a father is to his children"!

In the responses received, expressions identical or analogous to those of Liebniz were frequent. In a century when people live in a relationship of "management-property," when the relationships of "prince-subject" and "father-child" have undergone such grave revision, it can be understood how images conveying the idea of transcendence can themselves be sources of change, and perhaps deviation.

[13] Lalande, Vocabulaire technique et critique de la philosophie 1, 144.
[14] R. Jolivet, Metaphysique. 421–430.

This is especially true of adolescents breaking away from parental authority.

3. Pedagogical Perspectives

After this analysis of the difficulty, it is still necessary to speak somewhat at length of orientation of teachers. We shall dwell mainly on three key educational motifs, namely the catecheses on creation, on God's transcendence, and on the spirit of sonship in covenant with Jesus Christ.

Catechesis on Creation

Catechesis on creation must be Christian and not materialistic. In particular, catechesis must extol man's dignity as well as God's.[15] The aim in catechesis on this subject should be to show young people that the glory of God is manifested in the life of man.

The teacher should stress God the Creator, and not God as the master who one day established what he wanted; the teacher should show God as a person who eternally calls men to converse with him, a conversation which "personalizes" men and leads them to a true freedom. God should be presented as source of *life*, that is, source of a freedom creative of initiative. The teacher should know in particular that God is "happy" when man lives, when he builds, and when he marks the world with his personality.

[15] Otherwise it would be termed a "so-called" exalting catechesis of God. For one cannot extol the grandeur of God to the prejudice of man!

There are certain factors which must be stressed, such as whatever might concern God's "justice" and "jealousy." A just God does not desire that men go to hell, but that they be great with all the grandeur of freedom and communion.

The Bible shows creation as God's constant action, as a confrontation and battle so that life will emerge from chaos, so that realities will have meaning, rise out of the indeterminate and become, in their turn, "living and fertile beings." At a time when men are so conscious of creative freedom, it is evident that our teaching of the Christian meaning of creation must be more relevant.

Catechesis on God's Transcendence

The adolescent's familial crisis or his estrangement from the family is an excellent occasion for proclaiming and extolling the true transcendence of God the Father.

Reading the gospel, one notes how conscious Jesus was of all that touched the transcendence and glory of his Father. Perhaps because teachers have not sufficiently understood how to sympathize with adolescent aspirations, or because they have not been sufficiently conscious of the true values of the gospel, the spontaneous reaction or spirit of anger peculiar to biblical thought the moment someone tries to enclose God in terrestrial forms has been lost.

It would be well, not to mention liberating, for adolescents to see teachers not only uniting, but also dissociating God the Father from his human extensions and images. No, the bell which sounds at the end of class is not God the Father! No, the way a certain head of state or the head of some institution rules does not annex the authority of God the Father!

It would also be good to recover a certain touchiness when faced with those questions young people often pose with a subconscious insolence which tend to place God on trial. "Why did God make the world this way? "—Who are you, O man, to argue with God?" responds St. Paul (Rom 9:20). Again, we do not judge others. *Only God* can judge. We do not ask the date of the end of the world. We have not been placed above God to supervise his plan! And positively, especially in liturgical prayer, we must learn to ask for a certain patience, a seriousness, an attitude in which faith is expressed.

Teachers should be concerned with a whole educational system, a way of speaking and reacting which ceaselessly asks if one will be faithful to Jesus, "the one teacher" who truly taught who the Father is.

CATECHESIS ON THE SPIRIT OF SONSHIP IN COVENANT WITH JESUS CHRIST

The grave lacuna that exists on this point has already been discussed. In this section, one of the fundamental reasons why young people so often do not accede to an understanding of a mystery which seems to be very much in line with their sentiments will be discussed.

The Christian mysteries, the incarnation for example, can hardly be understood by young people when they are presented as entities cut off from the adolescent's life.

Perhaps this is one of the major reasons why the great
revealed dogmas actually remain exterior to the adolescent's thought and life, even after years of religious teaching. Their importance for life has never really been considered. And this is one of the essential points for
catechesis: adolescents apprehend a religious reality when
they become conscious of the transformations accomplished in them by this reality.

If young people are to understand that they are sons of
the Father in Jesus Christ, they must consider the *transformation accomplished in their life* by the covenant, and
this on all levels. In teaching prayer, for example, the catechist could first of all analyze "pagan prayer," its worth,
its courage, its difficulty, its tragic or even desperate tone.
Next he could concretely consider the prayer of a non-
believing man faced with death, or again, the questioning
of a Marxist. If the teacher were to ask why a pagan's
prayer is tragic or despairing or why a Marxist questions the
meaning of death, young people will say they do not understand how anyone can pray to an unknown and imper-
ceptible God. Then the catechist can point to the "believer," he who is with Jesus Christ and possesses the Spirit
of the Father. He can show that prayer and the life of the
Christian are renewed by certitude, the courage to speak,
familiarity, etc.

This example illustrates methodological development
and its adaptation to an adolescent mentality. Here the
incarnation is not presented as an abstract objective proposition, but as a proposition related to subjective experience,
aiming to encounter and transform this experience.

It has never been so important to bring forth a true understanding of creation and divine paternity as it is in our time, when man's creative power over the world is so forcefully expressed.[16]

And it is never so necessary to reconsider the Father who made heaven and earth as it is during adolescence when the earthly father is reconsidered.[17]

The crisis of understanding between the ages of 15 and 25 must not be neglected if childish anxieties are to be warded off and the adolescent is to surpass his revolts against the masks behind which the world hides God. But without a teacher who is himself very Christian and clear in what he believes, the adolescent will find it difficult to make the necessary breaks and purifications so that he will finally be able "to hear God, upright, and free of props."[18]

This generation believes in facts. The Church that young people encounter in their parents and teachers should be the sign and unimpeachable *fact* of the true God, a fact which urgently says to everyone: it is only in the Church that you will find a fact which so reveals *God's excellence* and *man's grandeur*. It is only in the Church that you will find a God so necessary and considerate of your freedom.

These considerations sum up an apologetic for our times. But how necessary it is that teachers reflect on the risks of being engulfed by human analogical experience and thus rise above the likenesses of the God of theodicy.

---

[16] See on this subject, R. Guardini, *Welt und Person*, all of the first part. See also his *The End of the Modern World*, New York 1956.

[17] See in particular J. Lacroix, *La révolte contre le père.*

[18] St. John of the Cross, *Dark Night of the Soul*, tr. E. Allison Peers, New York 1959, 55ff.

4. THE RELIGIOUS POSSIBILITIES OF ADOLESCENTS

N B

Everyone matures in stages. The object of genetics is the study of the value of these different stages, their significance and their relationships. The particular progress of each state is studied, showing how it constitutes a perfection of an earlier stage and how, despite its shortcomings and incompleteness, it is a preparation for the following stage.

Now that we are nearing the end of our study, we shall attempt to specify the purpose of adolescence from the perspective of a religious genetics. What progress has there been since the last stage? And how is adolescence evolving toward the next stage?

1. The Value of a Sensitive Period on the Religious Level

Before presenting the reader with these final conclusions, it would be valuable to specify, on the religious level, the value of the sensitive period.[1] This is an important question for the Christian teacher.

[1] By "sensitive period" is meant the stage in which the subject is inclined to a particular attainment, by virtue of a maturation of the functions necessary for this attainment. Thus, during childhood there is a period sensitive to learning to speak. This is the age when the child, spontaneously and easily, learns to speak.

What is the relation between human experience and faith, between a sensitive period and understanding of the faith? For example, what is the relation between the adolescent's experience of friendship and his understanding of the faith?

Teachers often answer unhesitatingly that human experience is a step on the road to a corresponding religious attainment. This is true, but it is ambiguous. What exactly does this answer mean? Does it mean that a religious attainment will spontaneously result from human experience? Does it mean that human experience is absolutely necessary for a religious attainment, and that as a result one cannot teach anything on the level of faith that does not correspond to some human experience? Does it mean that on the level of Christian life, a human experience is the stimulus for a corresponding life of faith?

Such questions certainly merit development and precision. Here only two points which seem most important to the subject will be stressed.

1. *Necessity of Human Experience for an Understanding of the Faith.* In responding to the questions posed, the following general principle will be adopted: one can have no *explicit* and *conscious* understanding of any aspect of the Christian message unless he has a *human experience analogous* to it. For example, a person only has an explicit understanding of supernatural friendship with God in Jesus Christ through the mediation of a human experience of friendship.[2] The key term is "*explicit understanding.*" Of

---

[2] Here we are speaking of an ordinary understanding of faith in Christian life, leaving aside the mystical phenomena related to extraordinary or miraculous cases.

course, it is evident that one can *implicitly* know and live the covenant in Jesus Christ without a human experience of friendship. But an explicit understanding would be impossible without the mediation of an analogous human experience.[3]

This principle is merely an application of natural laws of human understanding to the understanding of faith. Nothing can be clearly known and expressed that has not traveled the road of a human experience, at least an analogous one. Man can have no pure ideas.

Importance of This Sensitive Period. Such an assertion is full of consequences not only for an understanding of God, but for Christian life as well. Because religious realities cannot be explicitly known and lived in their full depth and meaning unless they correspond to a human experience, or at least to some more or less analogous human understanding, sensitive periods are especially opportune for the growth of faith.

They are opportune periods for two reasons:

First of all, on the level of understanding, faith finds analogies to clarify itself and words to express itself in human experience.[4]

On the other hand, on the level of daily life, the subject is motivated to discover the spiritual meaning of his human experience, and he is disposed to live better, precisely be-

---

[3] By "explicit understanding" we mean an understanding sufficiently conscious to be expressly stated.

[4] Certainly this does not obviate the need for a teaching or education aimed at explicit knowledge. But the catechesis of the covenant, for example, can be more adequately expressed through the analogy of friendship.

cause his experience reverberates deep within his personality.

Relativity of the Sensitive Period. However, the importance of sensitive periods should not be exaggerated, nor should they be considered absolutely necessary for every form of understanding. Again, there are two reasons for this.

First of all, it is possible to acquire a certain understanding of faith as the result of some early human experience which in its originality was comprehensive and already implicitly contained all others. Actually the child's human experiences already contain, in germ, experiences which develop later. In his filial and a fortiori fraternal relations, for example, the child already achieves (in a dull and incomplete, but real way) some dimension of friendship.[5] Thus a matter of faith which could not be explicitly known in childhood can nevertheless, in some way, already be attained. In this manner the young child can acquire a *certain* understanding of the covenant in Jesus Christ.[6]

On the other hand, the experiences of a sensitive period endure, and on the level of faith it will sometimes be much later that one will know what he had already learned on the

[5] Here we are distinguishing between filial love and the love of friendship. By friendship is meant a dimension of love characterized by reciprocity due to a certain equality and complementary aspect.

[6] But this understanding will not attain the conscious and explicit level it will attain during an age of friendship-experiences. We have noted with 11-year-old boys that the notion of covenant could be learned and in part understood, but in a different manner than with 16-year-old boys. At the age of 11 the notion of covenant tells them little. At the age of 16 it has profound resonances within their understanding and life.

level of human experience. Thus an explicit understanding of the covenant in Jesus Christ can be constantly developing.

2. *The Influence of Faith on Human Experience.* Human experience is essential for an explicit and conscious understanding of faith. However, the fact that faith, in its turn, influences *human experience* must be stressed.

This is true in the sense that understanding and the life of faith develop in man a clarity of vision and a strength and exigence.

The fact that a human experience is known and lived in faith leads to a perfecting, correcting and deepening of *its very human aspect.* Thus when friendship is lived and reflected on in faith, it will become more excellent and profound. On the other hand, this corrected and perfected friendship will make possible and call for a more explicit understanding of Christian life.

Here there is a veritable interaction, a reciprocal influence similar to the interaction of the intellect and will. It seems as if in all that happens the life of faith and human experience go together, aiding each other, each one putting its own riches and brilliance at the disposal of the other.

Thus far this discussion has concentrated on the role of human experience from a positive perspective. Certainly one should remember that human experience is, in itself, ambiguous and, even more, replete with possibilities for sin. If, in the positive sense, human experience favors a deepening of faith, it can on the other hand work against this tendency, making progress difficult and raising numerous obstacles. Nevertheless, for the teacher who knows how to correct and educate,[7] an age sensitive to certain human attainments is a time rich both in those experiences which favor an explicit understanding of the faith and in opportunities for perfecting the Christian life.

2. Two Areas of Progress during Adolescence

Let us now look at the progress proper to adolescence from the point of view of the religious sense and especially of the sense of God. What are the religious *possibilities* of adolescence? Basing the answer on the results of the investigation, *two types of progress* can be identified: progress related to the objective content of one's concept of God, and progress related to one's relationship with God.

1. *Progress Concerning the Content of One's Concept of God.* That which touches the objective content of one's concept of God will be discussed briefly. It is evident that maturation occurs in stages. In general, progress occurs on two levels:

—the adolescent acquires, in a sense which could be natural, a sense of *God's immanence;*

—the adolescent acquires, especially in late adolescence and young adulthood, a sense of *the incarnation* as God's personal covenant with man.

These are the two sensitive stages of progress, the first in some way underlying the second, and the second presupposing a Christian education and the openness of the subject.

The Sense of God's Immanence. The child acquires a certain consciousness of God's transcendence, a remote

---

[7] Educate, in the etymological sense of the word: to lead out of.

transcendence hidden in heaven, ruling all from above and "supervising" the course of things. This early consciousness of a God beyond and above the world continues to underlie the religious consciousness of adolescents. It is like an indeterminate essence. However, as late adolescence approaches, the progressive growth of a totally new concept can be verified. God is not only "above," he is "within," at the heart of the world. The adolescent discovers a new presence of God in man and in the universe. The adolescent has an acute sense of a superior power and intention inherent in things.[8] This evolution was analyzed in the discussion of symbolism and pseudo-pantheism.

Among the younger generations, the sense of immanence seems to be taking on new forms. Formerly, in a Platonic manner, man was conscious of the world as God's image. Thus romanticism's adolescent saw God in nature. Today there seems to be an evolution resulting from a more biblical orientation.[9] It is less a question of contemplating the static image of God than of being conscious of his "underground" action in the world's evolution and the projects of men. Thus for the adolescent there is interest not so much in reproducing God's image in himself as in "reproducing God's action," that is, in being faithful to God acting, creating and uniting all from the heart of the universe.

A Sense of God's Personal Covenant with Men. A sense

[8] On the forms of the sense of the sacred and immanence among adolescents today, see P. Babin, *Crisis of Faith*, New York 1964, 36–52.

[9] According to certain exegetes at least, "God created man in his image," that is, made him king of the earth to rule the animals and subdue the universe.

of the incarnation is not innate, it is revealed. Although it depends on the natural sense of God's immanence, it is definitely another matter. It is a sense of a God who enters historically and personally into each man's life, directing it to a goal infinitely beyond human possibilities. It could be said that a sense of the incarnation is based on the adolescent's experience and need for friendship, as well as on his need for a wonderful and successful future.

The adolescent says: my parents no longer interest me as before. I need a friend like me, to whom I can tell everything and who will shatter my solitude.

God says: I am sending my Son to be with you until the end of time, in an historical covenant relationship of personal friendship, not because you merit this, but because I love you.

Again the adolescent says: I want a wonderful and ideal future.

God says: I am sending you my Son so that henceforth you will desire nothing less than to enter into the glory of God. Live in faith in my resurrected Son. In him you have life and the certainty of a future resurrection.[10]

That adolescence is a time open to a sense of the incarnation can be clearly seen from the aforementioned points of departure. The child learned to say, Abba, Father! And the adolescent says in a special way, Lord, my Friend!

2. *Progress Related to the Mode of Understanding and*

---

[10] It should be noted that we have not written: "The adolescent says"—"God answers." The incarnation of God is not a response to the needs of man but a vocation to which man is called through God's mercy. The adolescent will never know the meaning of the incarnation without a Christian education.

Relation with God. The adolescent's progress regarding his understanding and relationship with God could be characterized by the term *"personalization."* This word sums up three realities which we shall study successively:

—access to his own vocation in his relations with God;

—access to a reflective consciousness in his relations with God;

—access to an autonomous personality in his relations with God.

Access to His Own Vocation in His Relations with God. By this is meant the particular way in which the adolescent knows and enters into relationship with God according to the characteristics proper to his own personality. Of course, God does not change. The plenitude of God's riches at once includes and transcends all the riches of the human spirit. What does change is the way in which man apprehends God and enters into relationship with him. Here one could distinguish the modes of understanding proper to man at different ages.

The child has a personal understanding, that is, an act of responsible knowing wherein he truly acts as subject.

But for the adolescent one should speak of *personalized understanding.* Here it is not only a question of an act of responsible knowing, but of an act of knowing which possesses characteristics and permanent differential modalities related to the subject's personality. One must remember the extremely varied nuances by which the adolescent expresses his relationship with God. As he nears young adulthood, the adolescent speaks less and less like the catechism, his parents or his milieu. He is becoming a person in his own right. His person is becoming personality.

He will speak, act and enter into a relationship with another according to the traits of his own personality.

In the Church, personality is called *vocation*. By this
is meant God's unique manner of calling man by his name
and man's absolutely singular and irreplaceable manner of
responding. It goes without saying that such a dialogue
with God is not simply by direct line, but includes a whole
gamut of fraternal and terrestrial relations which are also
dependent on the personality of each subject.

Thus the aim of the religious education of young people
should be to help them accede to their own vocation of
prayer and relationship in the kingdom of God.

*Access to a Reflective Consciousness in His Relations
with God.* At the age of reason the child has acquired a
psychological and moral conscience, that is, he considers
himself responsible and relates his acts to a norm of values.

Of the adolescent one could speak of a truly sensitive
stage not of conscience, but of *states of consciousness*. This
statement has a double sense. On the one hand, the adolescent *profoundly experiences* his own personality and his
relations with God, people and the world. And, on the
other hand, the adolescent *reflects* on what he experiences.

This reflection will profoundly affect his relationship
with God and his whole religious life by giving him a characteristic of interiority, seriousness and even a critical spirit
lacking at an earlier age. This progress does not really appear until late adolescence and young adulthood, when
the adolescent surpasses the simple and affective "pam-
pering" of his ego and awakens to reflective consciousness.
At the age of 15 the adolescent is happy to look compla-
cently at what he experiences, but he does not go beyond

the stage of affective "pondering." Between the ages of 18 and 20 this pondering is intellectualized. The adolescent analyzes, distinguishes, coordinates and criticizes the relation of what he experiences to what he has been and what the world has told him. He also thinks about what could be in comparison to what is.[11] This is an age open to faith. It is an age when the understanding of God and the religious life can be criticized, purified, enlarged or, in a word, personally reflected on.

Access to an Autonomous Personality in His Relations with God. This point is closely linked to the preceding, and characterizes above all the level of voluntary involvement in one's adherence to God. When we speak of an autonomous personality, we are thinking of one whose acts are disengaged from excessive outside control and from the overly spontaneous actions of childhood.

Excessive Outside Control. The adolescent is partially freed from the familial guardianship which directed his life and especially from the subconscious image this had left in his psyche and which expressed itself in tyrannical needs—the need for security, for example.

Overly Spontaneous Actions. Because of his reflective and now better characterized personality, the adolescent

[11] B. Inhelder and J. Piaget, *The Growth of Logical Thinking from Childhood to Adolescence*, New York 1958, ch. 6. Piaget speaks of formal thought, meaning a thought which, in order to resolve a problem, "begins full force by constructing an ensemble of hypotheses." This thought is capable of establishing processes of multiple and hypothetical combinations, and thus capable of subordinating the real to the possible. The adolescent asks: "Why did God make the world this way?" and his thought, "thrown out of gear" by several basic facts, tends to construct another world conceived according to his own norms. We stress how much such thought can push the adolescent to question religion.

places a certain interval, not so much temporal as existential, between demands from without and his response to them.

In a word, this is an autonomy which makes a decision either to reject or to integrate these demands. Simone de Beauvoir has said: "I became conscious of the inanity of the God of nature and I crossed God out of my life." The Christian approaching adult faith says: "I am consciously depending on faith in Christ for the outcome of my life."

According to the opinion of many psychologists, the final point of religious evolution is *conversion*. Conversion may be defined as:

> . . . the act or event in which the young person gives his life a direction and meaning in relation to transcendent values, with a depth of consciousness and decision that put an end to the vacillations of his adolescence and profoundly affect the moral and religious sense of his adult life.[12]

3. Toward Adulthood

The evolution toward adulthood is already evident, in seed, in the maturation of late adolescence. At this age there is a return to a sense of God which is more involved, more in accord with the demands of reason and the social group. The following seem to be the two most important elements in evolution toward adulthood.

1. *The Social and Ecclesial Element.* The young adult progressively enters into activity in the name of God. Thereby he is confronted with an historical situation to which he little by little will give his life.

[12] *Crisis of Faith*, 60.

2. *Objective Element.* Having discovered his God, man will more and more enter into relations with God which will be faithful to all the objective dimensions of revelation. In his thought and life he will enter into the trinitarian dimension of the mystery of God. But before this, there is the long road of young adulthood consisting above all in perfecting a personalized covenant life with Jesus Christ, in purifying and stabilizing the attainments of adolescence.

Besides childhood and perhaps old age, is there any age both so rich and so dangerous as adolescence for entering into an understanding of the true God? This is a period rich with a forceful call which bursts through excited natural tendencies. It is a period rich with new possibilities opening up to the young person for purifying the caricatures and false images of God which sleep within him. And it is an ambiguous period with its dual dangers of imprisonment in a natural context, and the hazards of a nature weighted with sin.

Such is the adolescent God has created. He must pass through this conflict and this painful growth finally to become an adult in the faith.

Perhaps one could apply to the adolescent what St. Paul said to the Athenians: "I see that you are in all regards the most religious of men." But at the same time, at a time when young people tend to approach the unknown God too naturally, how important it is that the true face of God who has raised Jesus Christ from the dead be revealed to them.

BIBLIOGRAPHY

BABIN, P., *Crisis of Faith*, New York 1964.

BOSSARD, J.H.S., and BOLL, E.S., *Ritual in Family Living*, Philadelphia 1950.

——, *The Sociology of Child Development*, rev. ed., New York 1954.

CARRIER, H., *The Sociology of Religious Belonging*, New York 1965.

CASTER, M. VAN, *The Structure of Catechetics*, New York 1965.

CLARKE, E.T., *The Psychology of Religious Awakening*, New York 1929.

GESELL, A., and ILG, F.L., *The Child from 5 to 10*, New York 1946.

GREEFF, E. DE, *Our Children and Ourselves*, New York 1963.

GRENSTED, L.W., *The Psychology of Religion*, London 1952.

HAGMAIER, G., and GLEASON, R.W., *Counselling the Catholic*, New York 1959.

HOURDIN, G., *La nouvelle vague croit-elle en Dieu?*, Paris 1960.

INHELDER, B., and PIAGET, J., *The Growth of Logical Thinking from Childhood to Adolescence*, New York 1958.

PEARSON, G.H., *Adolescence and the Conflict of Generations*, New York 1958.

PIAGET, J., *The Moral Judgment of the Child*, Chicago 1952.

SKINNER, B.F., and HARRIMAN, P.L., *Child Psychology*, New York 1941.

1.

The following questionnaire, given in its entirety, is the one used in the inquiry, and is the one upon which our interpretations were made. See Chapter 1, note 1, for breakdown into age, sex and numbers of students used in the inquiry.

Please give the name and address of your school. Indicate also your age.

Please circle one of the following:
1. Boy — Girl.
2. I am attending:
   a. a public school;
   b. a vocational school;
   c. a parochial school.
3. When I made my first communion, I was attending:
   a. a private school;
   b. a public school.

Please study the following questions very carefully, and circle the answer which seems to apply to you the most. Or if the question requires it, write out your answer in five or six lines beneath the question.
1. For you, what is God?
2. When do you prefer to pray?
   a. in the morning and evening; before studying;

    b. when I need help, generally before any important decision that I have to make;

    c. . . . .

3. When you pray, which way do you pray the most often?

    a. I usually recite my own prayers;

    b. I recite prayers I already know.

4. What is the usual reason why you pray?

    a. the feeling that I owe everything to God, and that I must do something for him;

    b. that my effort will be useful to someone, that I am useful;

    c. sometimes only in order to put myself to the test.

5. At the end of vocations, you are asked to make an examination of conscience. Of the three actions listed below, which seems to you the gravest? Circle in order of importance, listing the gravest action first:

    a. to miss Mass on Sunday through my own fault;

    b. to steal a dollar from one of my friends;

    c. not to make an effort for two months to love God and my neighbor.

6. In your opinion, what makes an interesting religion class?

7. What do you find to be the greatest difficulties in living a Christian life?

8. What aids you the best in living a Christian life?

9. Here are some subjects that are commonly taught in religion classes. Read them carefully, then circle them according to the order of importance, listing first the subject you prefer the most:

    a. sacred history, the great heroes of the Bible;

    b. Jesus Christ, his life according to the Gospel;

    c. the history of the Church, the saints of the Church up until now;

    d. our life of prayer;

    e. the sacraments in the life of the Christian;

    f. the liturgy in the life of the Christian;

    g. how to be a good Christian (difficulties and orientations);

    h. Christ, the ideal man who shows us the way;

    i. vocation in life: marriage, religious life, priesthood;

    j. faith, hope and charity;

   k. role of priests and Christians in the Church; the Church and the world;

   l. the Christian confronting the modern world; role of the Christian in the world; social questions.

2.

The questionnaire below was our first working hypothesis; given to two hundred adolescents, it was later abandoned since it did not admit of any profound interpretation.

Below are fifteen phrases, each one signifying a way in which we can comprehend, "conceive" of God, give ourselves an idea of God. Thus, when one thinks of God, when one prays, when one has a certain idea of him, one "conceives" of him in one's own particular way. Please indicate which phrase corresponds best to the way in which you conceive God.

• If the phrase corresponds *perfectly* with the normal way in which you like to think of God, write the number 1 under column P.

• If it corresponds *fairly well* (less perfectly), write 2 under column FW.

• If it corresponds *well enough* (poorly, rarely), write 3 under column WE.

• If it does not correspond at all, insert 0 under Column 0.

	P	FW	WE	0
		(sample response)		
1. God is Jesus Christ, whose human and divine history is traced in the Gospels.		2		
2. God is the Friend to whom I confide all my dreams and hopes, my sorrows.				0
3. God is the Creator, almighty, infinite and holy.		2		
4. God is the Ideal whom I wish to reach out to, in his Light and his Absoluteness and his Infinity.				0
5. God is the one who rewards my good				

actions and who will one day chastise
me for my sins.   3

6. God is the one who speaks to me from
the depths of my conscience, who
directs me.   2

7. God is the Confidant to whom I love
to speak in silence and repose.   0

8. God is the merciful and just Master
who demands of each according to the
talents he has received.   3

9. God is the Father full of tenderness
who guides all men.   1

10. God is Jesus Christ, my leader, whom
I want to imitate and follow gener-
ously according to his inspiration in
me.   1

11. God is the summit of Clearness, of
Cleanliness and of Fidelity.   2

12. God is a very merciful Savior who has
pity on sinners.   1

13. God is "he who is," the Being par
excellence, sovereign master.   3

14. God is Jesus who came on earth as a
beggar, a worker, a prophet and a
savior.   3

15. God is the one who is present in me
through grace and whom I adore.   3

ST. JAMES INFORMATION CENTER
205 N. PACIFIC COAST HIGHWAY
REDONDO BEACH, CALIFORNIA
PHONE: 374-1964